Not Always Easy

Lessons Learned on Introducing New Defense
Capabilities in Japan

JEFFREY W. HORNUNG

Prepared for the United States Indo-Pacific Command
Approved for public release; distribution is unlimited

NATIONAL DEFENSE RESEARCH INSTITUTE

For more information on this publication, visit **www.rand.org/t/RRA1300-2**.

About RAND

The RAND Corporation is a research organization that develops solutions to public policy challenges to help make communities throughout the world safer and more secure, healthier and more prosperous. RAND is nonprofit, nonpartisan, and committed to the public interest. To learn more about RAND, visit www.rand.org.

Research Integrity

Our mission to help improve policy and decisionmaking through research and analysis is enabled through our core values of quality and objectivity and our unwavering commitment to the highest level of integrity and ethical behavior. To help ensure our research and analysis are rigorous, objective, and nonpartisan, we subject our research publications to a robust and exacting quality-assurance process; avoid both the appearance and reality of financial and other conflicts of interest through staff training, project screening, and a policy of mandatory disclosure; and pursue transparency in our research engagements through our commitment to the open publication of our research findings and recommendations, disclosure of the source of funding of published research, and policies to ensure intellectual independence. For more information, visit www.rand.org/about/principles.

RAND's publications do not necessarily reflect the opinions of its research clients and sponsors.

Cover imge: Staff Sgt. Jessica Avallone/U.S. Air Force.

About This Report

The research reported here was completed in May 2023 and underwent security review with the sponsor and the Defense Office of Prepublication and Security Review before public release.

Japan and the United States are in close alignment regarding their threat perceptions of the regional security environment. This leads Tōkyō to see it in its national interest to host the largest number of U.S. forces of any country in the Indo-Pacific. Based on this fact, it is not uncommon to hear that Japan should host an even broader array of U.S. military capabilities. Although Tōkyō does have a strategic interest in hosting a robust U.S. presence, the assumption that Japan will acquiesce to any U.S. force posture is seldom explored in detail. This report examines this assumption by assessing the experiences of introducing new capabilities into Japan and establishing new bases there. The objective is to draw lessons on what the United States could possibly expect should it seek to introduce more-robust capabilities into the country. This report does so by examining previous instances of introducing new U.S. and Japanese capabilities and the construction of new bases in Japan. Collectively, these cases provide a broad spectrum of reactions that lead to several conclusions that can help inform the U.S. Department of Defense and U.S. Department of State on the possible range of responses to expect if Washington asks Tōkyō to host new, more-robust defense capabilities in the years ahead. These conclusions suggest that the: location of the capabilities matters; the type of capability may matter; central government agreement is a necessary but not sufficient condition to gain access for new capabilities; the size of the unit being deployed may matter; whether a capability requires a new base or can be deployed to an existing base may not matter in terms of obtaining access; and the level of local opposition appears to depend on how directly the local communities view the capability as affecting the peace, safety, and security of the community. Together, the overarching conclusion reached is that U.S. armed forces cannot assume that requests for deploying new capabilities in Japan will proceed smoothly or as planned because of the critical role that hosting communities play in the central government's decisionmaking.

RAND National Security Research Division

This research was sponsored by U.S. Indo-Pacific Command and conducted within the International Security and Defense Policy (ISDP) Program of the RAND National Security Research Division (NSRD), which operates the National Defense Research Institute (NDRI), a federally funded research and development center sponsored by the Office of the Secretary of Defense, the Joint Staff, the Unified Combatant Commands, the Navy, the Marine Corps, the defense agencies, and the defense intelligence enterprise.

For more information on the RAND ISDP Program, see www.rand.org/nsrd/isdp or contact the director (contact information is provided on the webpage).

Acknowledgments

The author would like to thank the two formal reviewers for this report: Mike Mochizuki of George Washington University and Kristen Gunness of the RAND Corporation. Mochizuki, an expert of Japanese politics and security policy, helped tease out important nuances that were not clear in the draft. He also pushed the author to think about additional factors that were not initially covered. Gunness, leveraging her broad expertise in U.S. security policies in the Indo-Pacific region, provided critical comments on how to clarify the linkages between the supporting evidence and the findings presented. This report is stronger because of their critical comments.

Contents

About This Report iii

CHAPTER 1
Introduction 1

CHAPTER 2
Reactions to New Capabilities and Facilities 3
   Reaction to New Capabilities 3
   Reaction to New Bases 14

CHAPTER 3
Conclusion 35
   Key Takeaways 35
   Recommendations 38
   Closing 40

Abbreviations 43
References 45

Introduction

As strategic documents released in December 2022 by Tōkyō reaffirm, Japan is a close U.S. ally, and the two countries are in alignment regarding their threat perceptions of China, North Korea, and Russia.[1] Therefore, Tōkyō sees it in its national interest to host the largest number of U.S. forces in the Indo-Pacific. Based on this fact, it is not uncommon to hear security and defense experts argue that Japan should host a broad array of U.S. military capabilities or acquiesce to hosting any U.S. force posture—even more-robust capabilities that are not currently on the archipelago.[2] These claims, however, are assumptions or, at best, optimistic expectations. Although Tōkyō has a strategic interest in a robust U.S. presence, its political leaders face local communities that host U.S. forces and need to balance their strategic interests with those domestic audiences. While outright refusals are rare, domestic opposition to U.S. presence often compels Tōkyō to request changes or cause delays to U.S. plans.

The Japanese government, therefore, must balance alliance ties and a robust U.S. military presence with meeting the demands of Japanese constituents asked to host U.S. forces. While it is true that the central government is the primary actor responsible for making national security decisions

---

[1] Cabinet Secretariat, *National Security Strategy of Japan*, Government of Japan, December 16, 2022; Ministry of Defense, *National Defense Strategy*, Government of Japan, December 16, 2022c.

[2] Sugio Takahashi and Eric Sayers, "America and Japan in a Post-INF World," *War on the Rocks*, March 8, 2019; Thomas G. Mahnken, Travis Sharp, Billy Fabian, and Peter Kouretsos, *Tightening the Chain: Implementing a Strategy of Maritime Pressure in the Western Pacific*, Center for Strategic and Budgetary Assessments, May 23, 2019; J. B. Vowell and Kevin Joyce, "The U.S. Army Can Be the Joint Force's Contact Layer in the Pacific," *Defense One*, January 9, 2023.

for Japan and, thus, the target audience of any U.S. request for introducing new capabilities, the political necessity of elected leaders in Tōkyō to address the concerns of local communities will always play an important role in responding to requests. This means that persuading Tōkyō to agree to hosting new capabilities, or implement force posture changes, can sometimes take a significant amount of effort and time.

Using publicly available articles and documents, including those by opposition groups, this report examines examples of new capabilities introduced in Japan by both U.S. forces and Japan's Self-Defense Forces (SDF).[3] The objective of this report is to examine the experiences of introducing new capabilities in Japan to draw lessons on what the United States could expect in the future should it seek to introduce more-robust capabilities into the country. The cases relating to new U.S. capabilities on existing bases include the construction of a Patriot missile storage facility, deployment of the Army/Navy Transportable Radar Surveillance system (AN/TPY-2), and the deployment of the MQ-9 Reaper. The case relating to new Japanese capabilities on existing SDF bases pertains to the introduction of V-22 Ospreys and the Aegis Ashore ballistic missile defense system. The report also examines examples of establishing new bases, such as U.S. efforts to relocate the Futenma Marine Corps Air Station in Okinawa, Japan's establishment of new SDF bases in the Nansei Shotō (southwest islands), and joint efforts to establish a facility on the island of Mageshima. The cases provide a broad spectrum of reactions, leading to several lessons that can help inform the U.S. Department of Defense (DoD) and U.S. Department of State (DoS) on the possible range of responses to expect if Washington were to ask Tōkyō to host new, more-robust defense capabilities in the years ahead.

---

[3] Because many Japanese articles are behind paywalls, the author had to rely on contemporary articles in English, which are not usually behind paywalls. Where possible, the author used primary Japanese sources. Japanese author names for Japanese language sources are cited family name first, followed by given name.

CHAPTER 2

Reactions to New Capabilities and Facilities

Japan's responses to introducing new defense capabilities and establishing new bases have not been consistent. They have ranged from absolutely no opposition, allowing smooth implementation; to some opposition but still allowing implementation, albeit sometimes different from the original plan; to opposition that results in the cancelation of the original plans. Examining Japan's responses to the introduction of both new U.S. military and SDF capabilities and bases therefore offers several useful insights.

Reaction to New Capabilities

No Opposition: Patriot Missile Storage Facility

One example of a U.S. request that apparently faced no opposition was the construction of the first U.S. Patriot missile storage facility at Kadena Air Base in May 2021.[1] The facility, meant to store Patriot missiles and facilitate rapid access to meet critical requirements related to air and missile defense operations, consists of a new reinforced concrete storage facility located in the munitions storage area on the base that is capable of storing 200 missile canisters.[2] It measures 1,700 square feet and has two main buildings designed to support separate missile batteries, as well as a state-of-the-art

---

[1] Daniel Andrews, "New Patriot Missile Storage Facility Unveiled in Okinawa," U.S. Army, May 24, 2021.

[2] SSFM International, "Patriot Missile Storage Facility," webpage, undated.

cooling and humidity monitoring system.[3] Both before and after its completion, there appeared to be no public opposition despite it being the first of its kind for U.S. forces in Japan.

This case is different than when the United States deployed its first Patriot system to Okinawa in 2006. Opposition from both then–Governor Inamine Keiichi and the public was strong.[4] Despite this initial opposition, over the years, it appears to have disappeared. It is unclear why the opposition disappeared, but the Japanese Ministry of Defense (MOD) made a concerted effort to convince the local community that the Patriot system would have no adverse effects on residents, cattle, or agricultural products; the MOD also argued that no live-fire training would take place on Okinawa and no expansion of the base would be needed.[5] These arguments appear to have worked because the original plan to create the storage facility for the Patriot system was signed in 2010, and there does not appear to have been any opposition.[6] Construction began in 2020 as a joint and bilateral project between Japan District, U.S. Army Corps of Engineers; 38th Air Defense Artillery Brigade; U.S. Air Force 18th Munitions Squadron; and Japan's Nishimatsu Construction Company. Although it is unclear why the project took ten years to begin, its completion appears to have occurred with no opposition.

Opposition but Implementation: Deployment of the Army/Navy Transportable Radar Surveillance System

Sometimes opposition exists but never creates enough momentum to affect the plan. An example of this is the U.S. deployment of the AN/TPY-2.

---

[3] Tong Ong, "US Army Opens Patriot Missile Storage Facility in Japan," *Defense Post*, May 26, 2021.

[4] Ministry of Foreign Affairs (MOFA), "Deployment of U.S. PAC-3 to Kadena," Government of Japan, July 20, 2006b; Chiyomi Sumida and Megan McCloskey, "U.S. Confirms Patriot Missiles Will Go to Kadena," *Stars and Stripes*, July 16, 2006.

[5] Sumida and McCloskey, 2006.

[6] Daisuke Sato, "U.S. Army Opens Patriot Missile Storage Facility in Japan," *Defence Blog*, May 26, 2021.

Because of the increasing missile threat from North Korea throughout the early 2000s, Washington and Tōkyō wanted to establish, and then strengthen, their ballistic missile defense systems. As part of this effort, the United States asked to deploy a second AN/TPY-2 radar in Japan to more precisely track the trajectory of missiles fired from North Korea. The radar system is composed of four mobile components: an antenna unit, an electronics unit, a cooling unit, and a prime power unit.[7] The plan was to deploy the system to the Air Self-Defense Force (ASDF) base of Kyōgamisaki in the city of Kyōtango, along with roughly 160 U.S. military personnel. Importantly, the system was to require the acquisition of several hectares of land. Although one such system was already installed in 2006 at the ASDF Shariki base in Tsugaru City in Aomori prefecture in northern Japan, the Kyōto radar represented the first such radar to be installed in the Kansai region of Japan.

The plan, announced publicly in a joint statement between U.S. and Japanese leaders in February 2013, immediately mobilized local opposition.[8] Citizens in Kyōto established a group to protest the plan, and about 250 people took part in an initial meeting.[9] Less than six months later, then-governor of Kyōto, Yamada Keiji, officially endorsed the installation of the radar, but told Tōkyō that he would rescind his endorsement if the central government failed to honor a pledge to ensure the local community's safety and counter electromagnetic interference and noise.[10]

Local opposition continued even after construction began at the site in May 2014; one report stated that more than half of the population of the district where the system was to be located opposed the plan.[11] This opposition was due partly to how the central government handled communications

---

[7] "U.S. Bolsters Missile-Defense Presence in Japan," Military.com, December 26, 2014.

[8] The two leaders confirmed an additional deployment of an AN/TPY-2 radar in Japan (MOFA, "Japan-U.S. Summit Meeting," Government of Japan, February 22, 2013a).

[9] "Kyoto Residents Organize to Block Installation of U.S. Missile Defense Radar Site," *Japan Press Weekly*, May 24, 2013.

[10] "Kyoto Agrees to Let U.S. Install X-Band Radar in Kyotango," *Japan Times*, September 20, 2013.

[11] "Local Residents Don't Want US Military Base to Be Built in Kyoto," *Japan Press Weekly*, October 5, 2014.

with the community and partly by the concerns of the local residents. Of the former, it was reported that the MOD went forward with the plan without informing residents in advance of the commencement of construction work; rather, residents were informed one day prior to the start of construction, which angered them.[12] Of the latter, residents were concerned by both the potential noise of the radar and the possible dangers the system may cause as it emits high-power electromagnetic waves. To obtain their approval, the central government organized 12 informational hearings for residents and, instead of expropriating the land for the U.S. military, arranged rental contracts with the landowners that were more lucrative than the market price.[13]

Although these efforts did not eradicate all local opposition, the two governments deployed the system in December 2014 as work continued on support facilities at the site.[14] Opposition by the local residents continued; complaints ranged from the low-frequency noise causing headaches or insomnia to fears the radar would make the area a target of attack.[15] In response to the complaints, the U.S. Army applied noise-reducing mufflers to the equipment in February 2015, which led to a decline in local complaints.[16] By October 2015, the work area was completed, and the required communications equipment was delivered and installed.[17] But logistical challenges delayed construction of the requisite living and relaxation areas until 2018. On March 1, 2022, all construction on those facilities was

---

[12] "U.S. Forcibly Begins X-Radar Construction in Kyoto," *Japan Press Weekly*, May 28, 2014; "Local Residents Don't Want US Military Base to Be Built in Kyoto," 2014.

[13] "Gov't Uses Power of Money to Have Residents Accept U.S. Radar Base Construction," *Japan Press Weekly*, May 11, 2014.

[14] DoD, "Second Missile Defense Radar Deployed to Japan," press release, December 26, 2014.

[15] Harumi Ishino, "Opposing U.S. 'Missile Offense' Radar Base in Kyoto," *Space4Peace* blog, March 26, 2015.

[16] Yun-hyung Gil, "Japanese Community with THAAD Radar Glumly Says 'It's OK,'" *Hankyoreh*, July 18, 2016.

[17] Bryan Duncan, "Army Signaleers Keep 14th Missile Defense Battery Connected," *PACOM News*, August 26, 2015.

finally completed, marking the end of construction that began in 2013.[18] On completion, there was no apparent opposition organized, and it is unclear whether opposition to the system continues.

Opposition but Implementation: MQ-9 Reaper

Another example of when opposition existed but failed to have any noticeable effect on the outcome was the U.S. plan to deploy MQ-9 Reaper drones to Japan.

In early 2022, media reports stated that Japan and the United States were considering a temporary deployment of seven or eight MQ-9 Reaper drones to the SDF's Kanoya Air Base in Kagoshima prefecture with the aim of strengthening vigilance and surveillance of Chinese activities.[19] The Reapers would be owned and operated by U.S. forces. In addition to the drones, initial reports said as many as 100 U.S. service members would deploy to the base.

Like previous examples, the initial announcement drew opposition from people living near the base who urged local officials to oppose the plan.[20] Not only did local opponents express concern about off-base incidents and accidents by U.S. personnel, but, like the previous examples, they feared the deployment would "threaten peace, safety, and security of the lives" of the residents.[21] Despite Kanoya having seen an increase in visits by U.S. military aircraft from Okinawa and Marine Corps Air Station Iwakuni, such as KC-130 tankers and Osprey tiltrotor aircraft, the proposed drone deployment was viewed as something qualitatively different. The view among opponents was that not only do U.S. MQ-9s carry weapons but also, as a

---

[18] Charlie Maib, "Kyogamisaki Communications Site: Knife Edge of Freedom," Defense Visual Information Distribution Service, March 7, 2022.

[19] "U.S. Spy Drones Likely to Be Deployed to Western Japan Air Base," *Japan News*, January 27, 2022.

[20] "Japan City Opposes Plan to Deploy Military Drones to Local Base," *Financial Assets*, February 5, 2022.

[21] Seth Robson and Hana Kusumoto, "Possible Deployment of US Reaper Drones Irks Residents of City in Southern Japan," *Stars and Stripes*, February 9, 2022a.

"weapon" that can be used to monitor and collect data on China, it "could make Kanoya a target."[22]

This opposition by the local community led the leadership of Kanoya to remain hesitant on accepting the plan, and an initial community meeting revealed residents' anxieties.[23] After several months of central government officials meeting with local residents, as well as an explicit statement that said the drones would be strictly limited to surveillance operations, temporarily deployed for one year, and that no weapons would be onboard the drones, Kanoya City mayor Nakanishi Shigeru approved their deployment in July 2022.[24] The first of an expected eight aircraft arrived at Kanoya in October 2022. While the timeline from initial announcement to deployment was surprisingly fast compared with other cases reviewed in this report, it is unknown whether the United States compromised on any part of its initial deployment plan. For example, it is unknown whether the United States initially asked that the drones be weaponized or whether it was hoping for a permanent rather than temporary deployment.

Opposition and Altered Implementation: Introduction of SDF V-22 Ospreys

Different from the previous three cases that examined U.S. capabilities on U.S. bases and where opposition either did not materialize or was largely minimized, opposition to Japan's deployment of V-22 Osprey tiltrotor air-

---

[22] Robson and Kusumoto, 2022a.

[23] "Kanoya, Voices of Complaint from Residents About the U.S. Military Unmanned Aircraft Deployment" ["鹿屋, 米軍無人機配備巡り住民から不満の声"], Kagoshima Yomiuri Terebi, February 15, 2022.

[24] For details on the efforts by central government officials meeting with local residents, both before and after the mayor's July decision, see "Information Regarding the Temporary Deployment of U.S. Military Unmanned MQ-9 Aircraft" ["米軍無人機MQ-9の一時展開に関する情報について"], Kanoya City, October 11, 2022; Seth Robson and Hana Kusumoto, "Reluctant Mayor OKs U.S. Military Drones in Southern Japan," Stars and Stripes, July 13, 2022b.

craft to its Ground Self-Defense Force (GSDF) in 2020 proved so problematic that the government was forced to change its plan.[25]

Initially, Tōkyō's plan was to deploy the GSDF Ospreys to Saga Airport in Saga prefecture. In 2014, Tōkyō approached Saga leaders to deploy 17 Ospreys from fiscal year (FY) 2019; the government planned to purchase land next to the airport in 2015 for the construction of new facilities.[26] That effort, however, ran into considerable problems because not only did Saga City officials oppose the plan but also local landowners, residents, and fishermen refused to allow the MOD to build new facilities on their plots, leading to protests and rallies to stop the move.[27] Their opposition mattered because the central government needed to obtain consent from the prefectural government and local fishermen who own the land. Without this, the government was unable to acquire the necessary land adjacent to the airport to build relevant facilities.[28] Saga Governor Yamaguchi Yoshinori, however, supported the plan, as did the Saga prefectural assembly and prefectural Chamber of Commerce, and they made efforts to persuade local residents who opposed the plan.[29]

---

[25] The case of the U.S. Marine Corps deploying its own Osprey tiltrotor aircraft to Japan is well known. The author initially wanted to include this as a case study, but surprisingly, it was difficult to find relevant data on the decisions behind its implementation and any potential changes in the implementation plan. Because these capabilities were deployed successfully, it would make an interesting companion case study to compare with the GSDF's experience.

[26] "Osprey, Provisional Use of Saga Airport Until Henoko Completion" ["オスプレイ、佐賀空港使用　辺野古完成まで暫定"], *Ryūkyū Shimpō*, July 23, 2014.

[27] "Saga Residents Protest Against Plan to Deploy Ospreys to Local Airport," *Japan Press Weekly*, July 23, 2014; "Saga City Disapproves of Use of Saga Airport for Ospreys," *Japan Press Weekly*, August 21, 2014; "Saga Citizens and JCP Protest Against Promotion of Osprey Deployment to Local Airport," *Japan Press Weekly*, July 5, 2017; "GSDF Ospreys Rejected by Saga Get 5-Year OK to Deploy in Chiba," *Asahi Shimbun*, December 25, 2019; "GSDF to Deploy Ospreys to Chiba as Fishermen in Saga Block Move," *Asahi Shimbun*, May 15, 2019.

[28] "Saga Residents Want Their Local Airport to Stay Free from Fisheries-Threatening Ospreys," *Japan Press Weekly*, July 27, 2017.

[29] "GSDF's Deployment of Ospreys to Saga Airport Likely Faces Delay," *The Mainichi*, July 19, 2017.

Because of the opposition, Tōkyō was forced to seek temporary alternatives to their deployment plan. While the MOD considered deploying the aircraft to Vice-Camp Takayūbaru in Kumamoto prefecture or temporarily storing them in the United States, it finally decided on temporarily deploying them to Camp Kisarazu in Chiba prefecture, considering the costs involved and the size of the facility.[30] But this too faced opposition by local residents in that prefecture and landowners who worried about the aircraft's safety record and worried that even a "temporary" deployment could eventually become a permanent deployment.[31] Following continued opposition by Chiba prefectural and Kisarazu city officials—for the same reasons—the MOD delayed the planned shipment of Ospreys that was scheduled to occur in fall 2018.[32]

As this was happening, in August 2018, Saga Governor Yamaguchi announced his intention to accept the Ospreys in Saga. Per the terms of his agreement with the central government, the MOD agreed to pay 500 million yen a year over 20 years (¥10 billion total; $93 million) to the prefecture as landing fees at Saga Airport for the Ospreys.[33] These funds, in turn, would be used to promote the fishery industry in the prefecture and support the local fishermen concerned about the impact the noise would have on their businesses.[34] This eventually led Kisarazu's city assembly and the mayor of Kisarazu to adopt statements stipulating that they would approve the temporary deployment if it were limited to five years; to which the MOD agreed, along with the assembly's requests to carry out a safety assessment of the

---

[30] "Japan Defense Ministry to Deploy Osprey Aircraft to Chiba Pref. Base," *The Mainichi*, March 27, 2018.

[31] "'Temporary' Deployment of JSDF Osprey Aircraft to Kisarazu Base Starts," *Japan Press Weekly*, July 11, 2020.

[32] Shinichi Akiyama, "GSDF to Delay Shipment of Ospreys to Japan as Local Opposition Mounts," *The Mainichi*, September 24, 2018.

[33] "Saga Pref. to Accept GSDF's Osprey Deployment," Nippon.com, August 24, 2018; Dylan Malyasov, "Japan Deploys New V-22 Osprey Aircraft to Chiba Amid Protests," *Defence Blog*, July 10, 2020.

[34] "Saga Pref. to Accept GSDF's Osprey Deployment," 2018; Malyasov, 2020.

deployment and to hold a meeting to discuss local residents' concerns.[35] Due to local opposition, however, the plans to build related facilities slowed.[36]

Despite this slow movement, in May 2020, the GSDF received its first delivery of an Osprey (originally planned for 2018), which was deployed to Kisarazu in July.[37] Despite the agreement reached in 2018 in Saga, implementation has proven difficult because negotiations between the prefectural government, the local fishermen, and the landowners have not been completed, which has led to the expectation that it will take several more years for the aircraft to be stationed in Saga.[38] As of March 2023, the Ospreys were still temporarily based in Chiba prefecture, not Saga prefecture as the MOD had planned, although it appeared that movement was building toward a solution.

Opposition Leads to Cancelation: Aegis Ashore System

Sometimes, local opposition has not just led to implementation delays, it has contributed to outright cancelation. Such was the case when Japan canceled its planned deployment of the SDF's Aegis Ashore ballistic missile defense system.

In 2017, Japan decided to purchase the Aegis Ashore system with plans to deploy two units at two separate GSDF bases: one in Akita prefecture in the north and one at Yamaguchi prefecture in the south. The plan was for the systems to be operational by the mid-2020s at the earliest. Their deployment was intended to provide an additional layer to Japan's existing ballistic missile defense (BMD) system. The sea-based tier, managed by the Maritime Self-Defense Force, consists of Aegis-equipped destroyers with interceptors, while the ground-based tier, managed by the ASDF, consists of fire

---

[35] "GSDF Ospreys Rejected by Saga Get 5-Year OK to Deploy in Chiba," 2019; "Kisarazu Mayor Gives Nod to 'Temporary' Deployment of Ospreys to Local SDF Base," *Japan Press Weekly*, December 26, 2019.

[36] Yoshitaka Ito, "SDF's 1st Osprey Force Deployed 'Temporarily' for 5 Years in Chiba," *Asahi Shimbun*, March 27, 2020b.

[37] "Japan Officially Takes Delivery of First Bell Boeing Tiltrotor Aircraft V-22 for Japanese Self Defense Force," *Navy Recognition*, July 2020; Malyasov, 2020.

[38] Akiyama, 2018.

units using the Patriot Advanced Capability-3 interceptor. This additional layer was to be owned and operated by the GSDF. Importantly, this system was strongly supported by the ruling Liberal Democratic Party, not least the then–Prime Minister Abe Shinzō, and reportedly by 66 percent of the Japanese population.[39] Yet, by 2020, the Japanese government announced it would cancel the planned deployment outright.

Like the previous cases, Aegis Ashore was opposed by local residents. While part of the opposition in Akita was due to the MOD having conducted an erroneous geographical survey in selecting the district as a candidate site, the overarching concerns at both sites were primarily fears of falling booster rockets, of becoming a target by hostile powers (i.e., a power at war with the United States or Japan), and radiation from the system's radar.[40] Despite the plan being supported by the ruling party and an initiative started by the then–prime minister, the government was sensitive to these local concerns, as residents mounted protests, voiced opposition against central government officials, launched signature campaigns, and pressured prefectural and local officials to oppose the central government's plan.[41] While the MOD held discussions with residents and officials over

---

[39] Tom Karako, "Shield of the Pacific: Japan as a Giant Aegis Destroyer," Center for Strategic and International Studies, May 23, 2018.

[40] "Japan to Talk with U.S. Over 180 Bil. Yen Aegis Ashore Deal," Kyodo News, June 16, 2020; "Japan Halts Deployment of U.S.-Made Missile Defense System," Kyodo News, June 16, 2020; Ishibashi Otohide, "Statement by Chairman Opposing the Deployment of Aegis Ashore in Araya Training Area" ["新屋演習場へのイージス　アショア配備に反対する会長声明"], Tohoku Federation of Bar Associations, July 12, 2019; "About the Resolution Regarding Opposition to the Deployment Plan to the GSDF's Araya Training Area of the Ground-Deployed Aegis System (Aegis Ashore) Which Threatens the Safety of Residents" ["住民の安全を脅かす陸上配備型イージス　システム（イージス　アショア）の　陸上自衛隊新屋演習場への配備計画反対に関する決議について"], Akita City, June 3, 2019; "About Information Relating to Aegis Ashore" ["イージス　アショアに関する情報について"], Akita City, undated; Thomas Lattanzio, "Aegis Ashore Cancellation—Impulsive Blunder or Strategic Opportunity?" Stimson Center, July 29, 2020.

[41] Shun Kawaguchi, "Signature Campaign Opposing Aegis Ashore Missile Defense System Held in North Japan," *The Mainichi*, December 16, 2019; Hayashi Kunihiro, "At the Town Meeting in Abu Town, Voices of Opposition to the Ground Aegis Deployment" ["陸上イージス配備に反発の声　阿武町で住民説明会"], *Asahi Shimbun*, December 21, 2019.

their concerns about the radar, they decided to cancel the deployment plan in Akita, moving instead to redo the geographical assessment at 20 potential sites in northern Japan.[42] But the MOD could not address the concern about falling boosters despite exploring the technical feasibility of whether it was possible to ensure the rocket boosters would fall away from residential areas and on the designated areas following separation from the missile. The government tried to modify the software on the interceptor missiles to ensure correct booster separation "so as to not put civilian lives and infrastructure at risk," but these efforts were not successful.[43] It was believed that this would cost $1.8 billion and take roughly a decade to fix, something the government did not support.[44] Despite the MOD promising since 2018 that it could ensure that the boosters would land in an SDF training area or the sea, narrowly selecting where the booster would fall would require a missile optimized for that specific feature, not the SM-3 Block IIA, which is optimized to have a longer range and a bigger warhead than previous interceptors.[45] Because it was not technologically feasible with the current interceptor, the MOD decided that the safety of the host communities could not be ensured without a costly and time-consuming hardware redesign, leading the government to suspend the deployment (and ultimately cancel its procurement).[46] Having given up on the land-based plan, in December 2020, the government began moving forward with an alternative to build Aegis Afloat ships, ships dedicated solely to BMD missions out at sea, away from local communities. Consideration of the ships' design was included

---

[42] Handa Shigeru, "Aegis Ashore, Big Contradiction in 'Review in Akita, Going as Planned in Yamaguchi'" ["イージス　アショア「秋田で見直し、山口は計画通り」の大きな矛盾"], *Gendai Business*, May 9, 2020; "Japan Scraps Aegis Ashore Deployment Plan in Akita," Nippon.com, May 6, 2020.

[43] Mike Yeo, "Japan Suspends Aegis Ashore Deployment, Pointing to Cost and Technical Issues," *Defense News*, June 15, 2020.

[44] Jeffrey W. Hornung, "Japan Is Canceling a U.S. Missile Defense System," *Foreign Policy*, July 2, 2020.

[45] Megan Eckstein, "Japan Officially Ends Aegis Ashore Plans After National Security Council Deliberations," *USNI News*, June 26, 2020.

[46] Mari Yamaguchi, "Japan Confirms It's Scrapping U.S. Missile Defense System," *Defense News*, June 25, 2020; "Japan Suspends Aegis Ashore Deployment," Arms Control Association, July/August 2020.

in the MOD's FY 2023 budget request, and media reports stated that a total of two ships would be completed by 2028.[47] As of March 2023, no apparent opposition to these sea-based ships have emerged.

Reaction to New Bases

The previous examples share a common theme of either the United States or Japan wanting to construct a new facility or deploy new capabilities to an existing base. As the examples show, there is no common pattern across the cases; as the cases resulted in different processes and outcomes. The next three cases are examples of when the United States and Japan, both separately and jointly, have tried to create new bases where none previously existed. Here, too, despite common patterns of opposition, there is no common pattern regarding the outcomes.

Almost 30 Years of Opposition Lead to Ongoing Challenges: Marine Corps Air Station Futenma (United States)

There are 76 U.S. bases throughout the Japanese archipelago, 31 of which are located in Okinawa prefecture.[48] This concentrated presence has historically drawn the most vocal opposition against U.S. presence compared with other parts of Japan. While the entire population of Okinawa should not be described as anti–U.S. presence—because pro-U.S. sentiment and support for U.S. bases do exist and possibly in larger numbers than Okinawa-based media polls show—public polls in Okinawa do show critical views of the United States and the U.S. presence. Polls taken prior to the 50th

---

[47] MOD, *Defense Programs and Budget of Japan (Overview of Budget Request for Reiwa Year 5)* [我が国の防衛と予算 （令和5年度概算要求の概要)], Government of Japan, August 2022b, p. 9; Narisawa Kaigo, "Ground-Based Aegis Replacement Ship, Consideration of Construction Costs in FY24 Budget and Commissioning at End of FY27" ["陸上イージス代替艦、24年度に建造費計上を検討27年度末就役へ"], *Asahi Shimbun*, September 2, 2022.

[48] MOD, "Areas of U.S. Forces Japan's Facilities, Zones (Exclusive Use Facilities)" ["在日米軍施設・区域(専用施設)面積"], Government of Japan, March 31, 2022a.

anniversary of the reversion of Okinawa, for example, show that 61 percent of people in Okinawa responded that the heavy U.S. military presence in Okinawa is "unequal" (compared with 40 percent nationwide).[49] A similarly high percentage of people stated that this concentration of U.S. forces in Okinawa is "discriminatory."[50] For those that oppose the U.S. presence, it is due to a mix of Okinawa's history of military involvement during World War II and subsequent U.S. occupation, environmental concerns, perceptions of discrimination against Okinawan people by mainland Japan, and complaints about noise and violence perpetrated by U.S. forces.[51]

Consecutive governors of Okinawa have called on Japanese and U.S. leadership to reduce the "suffering of excessive burden (過重負担の苦しみ)" placed on Okinawa by the presence of U.S. bases.[52] The current governor, Tamaki Denny, is like his predecessors in that he opposes the "extensive overconcentration of U.S. military bases in the prefecture," particularly on the main island of Okinawa where U.S. forces facilities and areas account "for about 15 percent of the total land area."[53] This large presence is viewed by Naha as "the biggest obstacle to the economic development of Okinawa," as well as the "incidents, accidents, aircraft noise, and other damages stem-

---

[49] "Base Concentration Is 'Unequal' in Okinawa Prefecture (61%), Different from 40% Nationwide, Shimpo/Mainichi Public Poll" ["基地集中は「不平等」沖縄県内61％全国 40％と落差新報 毎日世論調査"], *Ryūkyū Shimpo*, May 10, 2022.

[50] Respondents who "agreed" (39.4 percent) or "somewhat agreed" (26.9 percent) with this concentration being discriminatory were in the majority compared with those who "somewhat disagreed" (12.4 percent) and "disagreed" (10.7 percent). See Okinawa Prefecture Planning Department, "Figure II-2-76," in *11th Okinawa Prefectural Residents' Opinion Poll* [第 11回県民意識調査], March 2022, p. 83.

[51] Emma Chanlett-Avery and Ian E. Rinehart, *The U.S. Military Presence in Okinawa and the Futenma Base Controversy*, Congressional Research Service, R42645, January 20, 2016, p. 6; Olivia Tasevski, "Okinawa's Vocal Anti-U.S. Military Base Movement," *The Interpreter*, February 17, 2022; Sheryl Lee Tian Tong, "'Our Land, Our Life': Okinawans Hold Out Against New U.S. Base in Coastal Zone," *Mongabay*, November 25, 2021.

[52] "Looking Back at Governors' 'Peace Declarations,' with a Strong Sense of Anti-War and Base Issues" ["歴代知事の「平和宣言」を振り返る反戦、基地問題思い込め"], *Ryūkyū Shimpō*, June 21, 2019.

[53] Tamaki Denny, "Message from the Governor," Okinawa Prefectural Government Washington D.C. Office, undated.

ming from the U.S. bases" being a cause for adversely affecting the people of Okinawa.[54] Importantly, while the current governor says he agrees with national-level security arrangements, he finds it "absolutely unacceptable that Okinawa, which accounts for only 0.6 percent of Japan's total land area, hosts 70.3 percent of exclusive-use U.S. Force Japan facilities."[55] The consequence of this sentiment, shared by many prefectural residents, is that there is constant pressure on both Tōkyō and Washington to reduce the presence of U.S. forces on the island of Okinawa. This sentiment is best seen in the ongoing effort to close the Marine Corps Air Station Futenma and relocate it to the coast of Henoko in Nago City, another area within the island of Okinawa.[56]

Following the rape of a 12-year old girl by three U.S. servicemen in 1995, massive anti-base protests erupted in Okinawa, with estimates as high as 85,000 people.[57] In 1996, Governor Ōta Masahide (who had recently lost a lawsuit at Japan's Supreme Court concerning U.S. military presence in Okinawa), organized a nonbinding (first ever) prefectural referendum in which 89.1 percent of voters (with voter turnout at 59.5 percent) favored a reduction in U.S. bases.[58] Given the opposition, Tōkyō and Washington established the Special Action Committee on Okinawa (SACO) to discuss ways to alleviate the presence of U.S. forces on Okinawa. In April 1996, leaders of the two countries announced that Futenma would be closed and returned within the next five to seven years, after an adequate replacement facility was completed and operational.[59] Then, in December, the allies released the

---

[54] Tamaki, undated.

[55] Tamaki, undated.

[56] For background on the Futenma relocation issue, see Chanlett-Avery and Rinehart, 2016; Mari Yamaguchi, "Tens of Thousands Rally for Removal of Marine Base on Okinawa," *Marine Corps Times*, August 12, 2018; Mari Yamaguchi, "Okinawa Governor Renews Demand to Stop Marine Corps' Futenma Base Relocation Plan," *Marine Corps Times*, December 26, 2019.

[57] Sam Jameson, "Huge Rally in Okinawa Denounces U.S. Bases," *Los Angeles Times*, October 22, 1995.

[58] Andrew Pollack, "Okinawans Send Message to Tokyo and U.S. to Cut Bases," *New York Times*, September 9, 1996.

[59] MOFA, "The SACO Final Report," Government of Japan, December 2, 1996.

SACO report, which included an agreement to close Futenma at its current location and pursue a sea-based facility option.[60] The exact relocation site, however, was not specified (that was decided by a cabinet decision in December 1999).[61]

About seven months after the release of the SACO report, Ōta appeared to show his willingness to cooperate with Tōkyō on the sea-based option at a meeting with then–Prime Minister Hashimoto Ryūtarō in July 1997.[62] Then, following a Nago City referendum on the issue in December 1997, Ōta backtracked on his support and, by February 1998, once again opposed the sea-based option. The 1999 decision naming Henoko led local residents to begin a campaign to oppose construction of the offshore base, pointing to the threat it would pose to daily life and the environment, including both noise and crime.[63] This opposition, accompanied by protests and demonstrations, slowed progress for the next several years.

In 2006, the George W. Bush administration instituted the Defense Policy Review Initiative (DPRI) as part of its global posture review process. The DPRI's objectives were, in part, to realign the U.S. regional force structure and to relieve some of the tensions with local communities in Japan, given the ongoing opposition to the relocation plans. In October 2005, the two governments agreed to review "the posture of U.S. forces in Japan and related SDF forces, in light of their shared commitment to maintain deterrence and capabilities while reducing burdens on local communities,

---

[60] MOFA, 1996.

[61] Cabinet Office, "Government Plan Concerning the Relocation of Futenma Airfield" ["普天間飛行場の移設に係る政府方針"], Government of Japan, cabinet decision December 28, 1999, abolition May 30, 2006.

[62] "Contents of the Last Meeting, Mr. Hashimoto and Mr. Ota's 'Honeymoon,' Governor Looks Away as Prime Minister Pressures, 'It Was a Bizarre Atmosphere That Froze the Place'" ["その場が凍り付く異様な雰囲気だった」迫る首相にうつむく知事 「蜜月」の橋本・大田氏、最後の会談の中身"], Okinawa Times, March 13, 2022.

[63] Celine Pajon, "Understanding the Issue of U.S. Military Bases in Okinawa," Institut Français des Relations Internationals, June 2010; Steve Rabson, "Henoko and the U.S. Military: A History of Dependence and Resistance," Asia-Pacific Journal, Vol. 10, Iss. 4, No. 2, January 16, 2012.

including those in Okinawa."[64] Included in this initiative was the decision to reconfigure the facilities in the Camp Schwab area to accommodate the relocation of Futenma-related activities, making it the Futenma Replacement Facility (FRF).[65] Toward that end, the allies agreed in May 2006 that "approximately 8,000 III Marine Expeditionary Force (MEF) personnel and their approximately 9,000 dependents will relocate from Okinawa to Guam by 2014, in a manner that maintains unit integrity."[66] Important in their efforts to try to obtain local consent, the bilateral agreement included the construction of "two runways aligned in a 'V'-shape, each runway having a length of 1,600 meters plus two 100-meter overruns" at the FRF on landfill.[67] This runway specification was motivated, in part, by the expressed concern of local mayors who wanted to avoid air traffic flying over local villages (which an original L-shaped runway configuration would do).[68] Based on the agreement, an environment impact assessment was conducted, beginning in 2008.[69]

It should be noted that despite this agreement, the DPRI FRF plan was problematic from the start because it amounted to discarding a proposal initiated by the conservative governor Inamine Keiichi, who advocated a

---

[64] Security Consultative Committee, "U.S.-Japan Alliance: Transformation and Realignment for the Future," U.S. Department of State, October 29, 2005, p. 7.

[65] Security Consultative Committee, 2005, p. 11.

[66] Security Consultative Committee, "United States-Japan Roadmap for Realignment Implementation," U.S. Department of State, May 1, 2006; MOFA, "Concept Plan," image, April 28, 2006a.

[67] Security Consultative Committee, 2006.

[68] The mayors of Nago and Ginoza came to an agreement with the Minister of State for Defense on April 7, 2006, that the FRF plan would be based on an October 29, 2005 Security Consultative Committee) document and that the flight route should avoid flying over Nago and Ginoza by building two runways in a V shape. See Security Consultative Committee, 2005, p. 11. For an initial concept plan from the same period, see MOFA, "Reference," image, Government of Japan, undated.

[69] The assessment took three years, finishing in 2011. MOD, "Council on Measures Concerning the Relocation of Futenma Airfield (2nd Session)" ["普天間飛行場の移設に係る措置に関する協議会（第2回）"], Government of Japan, December 25, 2006; MOD, "Council on Measures Concerning the Relocation of Futenma Airfield (3rd Session)" ["普天間飛行場の移設に係る措置に関する協議会（第3回）"], Government of Japan, January 19, 2007.

joint military-civilian facility at Henoko. Although the Inamine proposal was opposed by some segments of Okinawa, the DPRI FRF concept of the two V-shaped landfill runways emerged without active involvement of local authorities and eventually presented to local authorities as a fait accompli developed between the U.S. and Japanese governments. The result was resentment, therefore, from the very start of the project.[70]

And yet, plans based on the agreement moved forward. As the environmental impact assessment was being carried out, Hatoyama Yukio became Japan's premier in 2009, promising to move Futenma off the island of Okinawa entirely. This led to a review of the processes, which led to the current site of the FRF, temporarily stalling movement. In May 2010, however, his administration officially reconfirmed the previous agreement, finding there were no other alternatives. Although he eventually resigned, his actions prior to his resignation reinvigorated those who opposed the Futenma relocation plan. For example, not only did the new Nago mayor, Inamine Susumu (elected in January 2010), openly oppose the plan, so did a growing portion of the public. In April 2010, more than 90,000 protestors in Okinawa turned out to oppose the Futenma plan.[71]

The opposition continued, slowing progress. The environmental impact assessment proceeded, and the final report was submitted to the Okinawa prefectural government in December 2011 (with a revised version submitted in December 2012). Then, in April 2012, Tōkyō and Washington adjusted the plans outlined in the 2006 agreement. This included delinking both the relocation of the III MEF personnel from Okinawa to Guam and resulting land returns south of Kadena Air Base from progress on the FRF.[72] They

---

[70] In addition to this resentment, there are rumors that construction interests in Okinawa might have backed the landfill project because of the economic benefits—leaving questions of corruption—and questions about the military utility of the FRF were fueled by a U.S. Government Accountability Office finding that the landfill FRF would not meet U.S. military operational requirements (U.S. Government Accountability Office, *Marine Corps Asia Pacific Realignment: DOD Should Resolve Capability Deficiencies and Infrastructure Risks and Revise Cost Estimates*, GAO-17-415, April 2017).

[71] Martin Fackler, "90,000 Protest U.S. Base on Okinawa," *New York Times*, April 25, 2010.

[72] Security Consultative Committee, "Joint Statement," Ministry of Foreign Affairs, Government of Japan, April 27, 2012.

also updated the number of marines to be relocated to Guam and decided that "a total of approximately 9,000 U.S. Marines, along with their associated dependents, are to be relocated from Okinawa to locations outside of Japan"; additionally, the "authorized strength of U.S. Marine Corps forces in Guam is to be approximately 5,000 personnel."[73] Importantly, they remained in agreement that the FRF, planned for the Camp Schwab-Henoko area and adjacent waters, remained the only viable solution. This led to the April 2013 Okinawa Consolidation Plan released by Washington and Tōkyō, which set forth the implementation plan—including sequencing steps—in accordance with the realignment roadmap agreed to in April 2012.[74] Then, in December 2013, Governor Nakaima Hirokazu approved the central government's landfill permit request, thereby allowing construction on the FRF to commence.

Despite this progress, local opposition once again affected progress. This construction delay began with Onaga Takeshi, Nakaima's successor since November 2014, revoking the landfill permit on October 13, 2015, freezing all FRF work.[75] In response, the very next day, the Okinawa Defense Bureau (the local branch of the MOD) filed a complaint with the Minister of Land, Infrastructure, Transport and Tourism (MLITT) to review the revocation and requested a stay of execution.[76] MLITT complied, suspending Onaga's cancelation order and ordering a stay of execution. This action resulted in a lot of back and forth between MLITT and the governor, leading ultimately to the central government suing the Okinawan governor seeking to overturn Onaga's decision to cancel the land reclamation approval.[77] The Okinawan

---

[73] Security Consultative Committee, 2012.

[74] MOFA, *Consolidation Plan for Facilities and Areas in Okinawa*, Government of Japan, April 2013b.

[75] Onaga Takeshi, "The Governor of Okinawa Revoked the Reclamation Approval for the New U.S. Base at Henoko on Oct 13th, 2015," Okinawa Prefectural Government Washington, D.C. Office, October 13, 2015.

[76] Takayoshi Igarashi, "Reclamation, Licensing, and the Law: Japan's Courts Take Up the Henoko Base Issue," trans. by Sandi Aritza, *Asia-Pacific Journal*, Vol. 14, Iss. 1, No. 2, January 1, 2016.

[77] Mari Yamaguchi, "Tokyo Sues Okinawa in U.S. Base Relocation Dispute," *Air Force Times*, November 17, 2015a; Mari Yamaguchi, "Okinawa Officials Sue to Stop Move of

prefectural government counter-sued the MLITT minister the next month, arguing that MLITT illegally suspended Onaga's cancelation.[78] Despite a March 2016 court-mediated settlement to stop construction work and for Tōkyō and Naha to resume negotiations, they did not proceed well.[79] By July, Tōkyō sued Onaga on the grounds that he acted illegally by revoking the land reclamation permit. In September, the Fukuoka High Court ruled in Tōkyō's favor, finding Onaga's action illegal.[80] Onaga appealed to Japan's Supreme Court which, in December 2016, ruled to dismiss the appeal and let the Fukuoka judgment stand; Naha complied by retracting the revocation of the reclamation approval, thereby allowing work to continue.[81]

By 2018, reclamation work had resumed, but it still faced continued opposition by Naha and a vocal segment of the population. In fact, in 2019, a public referendum (the first since 1996) resulted in 72 percent of voters in Okinawa opposing the relocation.[82] Because the referendum was nonbinding, construction continued, although Minister of Defense Iwaya Takeshi said, "we must take the will of the people reflected in the prefectural referendum seriously" at a press conference following the referendum.[83]

Marine Corps Air Station Futenma," *Defense News*, December 25, 2015b.

[78] "Okinawa Sues Tokyo in Latest Bid to Stop US Base Relocation," Voice of America, December 25, 2015.

[79] "Distrust Between Central Gov't, Okinawa Pref. Lingers Ahead of Court Talks on Futenma," *The Mainichi*, March 22, 2016.

[80] Chiyomi Sumida and Matthew Burke, "Okinawa Governor Loses Battle in Base-Relocation War," *Stars and Stripes*, September 16, 2016.

[81] Mieno Yasushi, "The System of Lawsuits to Confirm the Illegality of Inaction by the Government Against a Local Government" ["国の自治体に対する不作為の違法確認訴訟制度のあり方"], *Jichi Soken*, Vol. 467, September 2017; Kamiya Nobuharu, "Various Problems Regarding the 12th Henoko Litigation Supreme Court Decision" ["第12回 辺野古訴訟最高裁判決を巡る諸問題"], *LIBRA*, Vol. 17, No. 11, November 2017.

[82] There were three options in the referendum: support the move, oppose the move, or neither. Seventy-two percent of voters opposed the relocation, compared with 19 percent in favor and around 9 percent voting for neither. Voter turnout was 52 percent. See "Okinawa: Tokyo to Overrule Referendum on U.S. Base," BBC, February 25, 2019.

[83] MOD, "Minister of Defense Press Conference" ["防衛大臣記者会見"], Government of Japan, February 26, 2019.

As of this writing, despite continuing opposition, landfill work continues in the Henoko Bay area (south side), while work in Ōura Bay (east side) is pending approval of the landfill permit modification request submitted to the Okinawa prefectural government by the Okinawa Defense Bureau. The approval is necessary for the MOD to conduct seabed improvement work before undertaking reclamation work.[84] The Okinawa prefectural government disapproved the request in November 2021, and it is currently under administrative review. Meanwhile, both sides continue to institute various lawsuits against each other, including the one that originated from Naha's decision to withdraw the landfill permit in August 2018.[85] Despite nearly three decades since the initial plan to close and relocate Futenma, ongoing local challenges continue to slow efforts.

GSDF Bases (Japan)

While the construction of the FRF continues to prove difficult close to three decades since the initial agreement, a separate insightful example regarding the construction of new military bases is Japan's recent efforts to construct GSDF bases on four islands in the Nansei Shotō, the southwest island chain that stretches from southern Kyūshū throughout the islands of Okinawa prefecture down to the islands closest to Taiwan. Although the bases themselves are not large, they contain housing facilities, training grounds, and ammunition depots. Three of them—Amami-Ōshima, Ishigaki, and Miyako—also have ground-to-air and anti-ship cruise missile batteries. Available reporting shows that the latter two islands experienced fairly active opposition to the establishment of the bases; groups cited the dangers that the kinetic capability would mean for the island if China were to target them in an attack. The base that does not have missiles, Yonaguni, saw comparatively less opposition. Because very little data are available for

---

[84] There is no space to detail the issue here, but the soft seabed in deep waters on the eastern side of the FRF landfill has become a serious issue. Experts have indicated that even after the MOD's proposed improvements, the stability of the runways would be precarious.

[85] "Chronicles of the Relocation Problem (by Year)" ["移設問題の動向（年表）"], Nago City, undated.

the case of Amami-Ōshima, it is not examined below. The three cases that are examined are all islands in Okinawa prefecture.

Relatively Little Opposition: Yonaguni

The GSDF's first detachment was sent to Yonaguni in March 2016. The coastal surveillance unit is responsible for monitoring Chinese activity in the area and saw relatively little opposition to its establishment. As noted above, it remains the one island of the four where new GSDF bases were constructed that does not host any kinetic capabilities.

The idea to deploy troops to Yonaguni began around 2009; Tōkyō decided in 2011.[86] Based on residents' interest in the economic benefit that could occur from an SDF presence but fears such presence might prompt counter-measures by China, in September 2012, Yonaguni Island's town assembly voted 3 to 2 against a proposal to conduct a town plebiscite on the question of whether to host an SDF facility.[87] A supporter of the plan, island mayor Hokama Shukichi, won reelection in August 2013, after running on a pro-deployment campaign. Local residents, however, remained split. Supporters backed the idea that an influx of personnel could help boost the local economy and help keep the island safe from Chinese aggression.[88] Those who opposed were concerned about the negative health effects from the radar's electromagnetic waves, as well as the base making the island a target of attack if a contingency were to erupt.[89] In September 2014, opposition party members submitted a local referendum vote to decide the issue. The referendum was eventually held on February 22, 2015, and, contrary to the opposition's wishes, it passed 632-445 (with an 86-percent turnout rate), reflecting a division but nevertheless support for hosting the SDF.[90]

---

[86] Gavan McCormack, "Yonaguni: Dilemmas of a Frontier Island in the East China Sea," *Asia-Pacific Journal*, Vol. 10, Iss. 40, No. 1, September 30, 2012, pp. 8–9.

[87] McCormack, 2012, p. 10.

[88] Shannon Tiezzi, "Japan to Station Troops on Yonaguni, Near Disputed Islands," *The Diplomat*, April 19, 2014.

[89] Tiezzi, 2014; Mina Pollmann, "Japan Troop Deployment Near Taiwan Clears Major Hurdle," *The Diplomat*, February 25, 2015.

[90] Shogo Hara, "GSDF's Radars on China on Japan's Westmost Island Less Divisive 5 Years After Deployment," *Japan News*, March 28, 2021; Pollmann, 2015.

Those who supported the referendum stated that the island needed stronger defenses and that new residents could help bring extra money to the local economy, something that local leadership had reached out to the Defense Minister about in 2009, hoping that having troops stationed on the island could help slow depopulation and revive the economy.[91] This logic appears to have been correct because, despite the initial community division, as the GSDF members integrated into the local community and the tax revenues on the island increased, opposition to their presence has declined.[92]

Opposition Leads to Change: Miyako

Following the Yonaguni base deployment, similar units on Amami-Ōshima and Miyako were established in March 2019. While little information is available for the former, the evidence available for the latter suggests that the experience was less congenial than Yonaguni, largely due to the stationing of kinetic capabilities.

As with Yonaguni, the central government first expressed an interest in establishing a GSDF base on Miyako in 2011. Initial meetings in 2014 between government representatives were not problematic.[93] In 2015, media reported that central government officials had talked about two candidate sites and asked Mayor Shimoji Toshihiko about the island hosting surface-to-air and anti-ship cruise missiles.[94] In 2016, without the broad support of the local community, Mayor Shimoji announced his approval of the plan, thrusting the issue to the center of his reelection campaign in 2017, which he won despite local opposition.[95]

The MOD initially presented two prospective sites (Daifuku ranch and Chiyoda Country Club) where the GSDF could both build a base and house

---

[91] Pollmann, 2015.

[92] Hara, 2021.

[93] "Vice Defense Minister Requests Miyako Survey of GSDF Deployment" ["防衛副大臣、陸自配備で宮古島調査を要請"], *Ryūkyū Shimpō*, June 13, 2014.

[94] "Suggesting Approximately 800 SDF Personnel Deployed to Miyako, Meeting Between Vice Defense Minister Satō and Mayor Shimoji" ["宮古島に自衛隊約８００人配備打診　左藤防衛副大臣、下地市長面談"], *Ryūkyū Shimpō*, May 11, 2015.

[95] "Ex-Mayor Held in Bribery Case Tied to GSDF Camp on Okinawa Isle," *Asahi Shimbun*, May 13, 2021.

the ammunition depot. The mayor, however, ruled out the Daifuku site over concerns about potential water pollution; instead, he promoted the Chiyoda Country Club golf course, which was eventually chosen.[96] (Years later, it came to be known that his approval against local opposition was motivated by profit, and he was arrested on bribery charges for promoting the golf course as the MOD's only option.) Construction of the base began in November 2017, which elicited protest from opposition groups who were fearful that the GSDF base would make Miyako a target.[97]

Like the GSDF Osprey deployment detailed earlier in this chapter, this opposition caused the central government to slightly alter its plan. By March 2019, facilities to house the SDF personnel had been completed according to the original plan.[98] But local landowners continued to oppose the stationing of both the missile launchers and an ammunition depot on the base, forcing a delay in the construction of these facilities as the government and local officials sought to find an alternative site to house the depot.[99]

Those that opposed the depot complained that the facility was intended for the storage of ammunition of "small-fire equipment," not missiles; initially, the MOD only said that "rifle shots, smoke pots and other such weapons" would be stored at the base.[100] Other complaints included concerns that the ammunition depot was constructed too close to a residential area in violation of Japanese domestic law that regulates the safety area to 400 meters

[96] "Protest by Opposition Faction of Residents on Miyako to Full Start of Construction of GSDF Garrison" ["陸自駐屯地の本格工事に着手　宮古島市　反対派住民は抗議"], *Ryūkyū Shimpō*, November 20, 2017; "Ex-Mayor Held in Bribery Case Tied to GSDF Camp on Okinawa Isle," 2021.

[97] "130 Residents Protest the Start of Construction, 'No' to the GSDF Deployment to Miyako" ["宮古島陸自配備にノー　市民１３０人、着工に抗議"], *Ryūkyū Shimpō*, December 14, 2017.

[98] "Miyako GSDF, Government Starting Construction in January, Accelerating Work Toward Deployment" ["宮古陸自、1月着工　政府、配備に向け作業加速"], *Ryūkyū Shimpō*, October 16, 2017.

[99] "Defense Political Vice Minister Suggests Ammunition Depot in Bora Mine to Mayor Shimoji" ["保良鉱山に弾薬庫　防衛政務官が下地市長に打診"], *Ryūkyū Shimpō*, January 17, 2018; Ito, 2020b.

[100] Shinichi Fujiwara, "Clumsy Strategy Weakening Bid to Shore Up Remote Island Defenses," *Asahi Shimbun*, April 29, 2020.

and that the ground under the fuel storage site was not strong enough, leading to fears of potential leakage into groundwater.[101] Despite the base opening in March 2019, the local opposition to the depot forced an apology from the Defense Minister, a temporary removal of the trench mortar shells and other weapons that were already stored on the base from the island, and a delay in the construction of the munitions depot that was originally set to be completed in spring 2020.[102] The base was largely completed by March 2020, but it was different from the MOD's original intentions.[103] Instead of locating both the base and depot at the Chiyoda Country Club site, the MOD was forced to build the ammunition depot off site at the Bora mine.[104] That depot became operational in April 2020 and often is greeted by protestors whenever munition deliveries arrive. Google maps shows that the distance between the base and the depot is roughly 15 km.

Opposition but Thus Far, Little Impact: Ishigaki

Like the opposition experienced on Miyako, while different from the Yonaguni opposition, Ishigaki residents' opposition to the GSDF base was present from its beginning. The central government initially began conversations with Ishigaki leadership in 2015, which was favorably received by Mayor Nakayama Yoshitaka (despite not explicitly saying he supported the plan).[105] Even before the opening of the bases on Amami-Ōshima and

---

[101] Seiko Sakaguchi, "A Report from Miyako Island: What Is Happening on the Small Islands of Okinawa?" *EcoJesuit*, June 30, 2019; "Miyako Residents Request Defense Bureau to Halt Deployment of GSDF Missile Base as Construction Proceeds Without Ground Reinforcements" ["陸自ミサイル基地配備中止を　宮古島住民が防衛局要請　地盤改良せずに建設へ"], *Ryūkyū Shimpō*, August 27, 2019.

[102] Fujiwara, 2020.

[103] "Formation of Miyako Garrison Complete, GSDF 700 Person in Scale, Even Though Request Made to Postpone Due to COVID Measures, Ceremony Proceeded" ["宮古駐屯地の編成完了　陸自、700人規模　コロナ防止で延期要請も式典強行"], *Ryūkyū Shimpō*, April 5, 2020.

[104] "Local Residents Oppose Construction of GSDF Facility on Miyako from Early Morning, 'Don't Build a Dangerous Ammunition Depot'" ["「危険な弾薬庫造るな」宮古島の陸自施設着工　市民、早朝から抗議"], *Ryūkyū Shimpō*, October 8, 2019.

[105] "Missile Unit Also on Ishigaki, MOD Considering 2 Companies of 120 People" ["石垣にもミサイル部隊　防衛省、2中隊120人検討"], *Ryūkyū Shimpō*, May 13, 2015;

Miyako in March 2019, however, Ishigaki residents protested construction—particularly after it was made known that Nakayama supported the plan. Opposition focused on the dangers of Ishigaki being targeted in a conflict, as well as the potential damage to local industry because of the base.[106] In May 2017, a group of residents submitted to the MOD signatures accounting for 70 percent of island residents who opposed the GSDF deployment.[107] And two months before the March 2018 mayoral election, a local rally of 400 residents who opposed the GSDF plan highlighted the ongoing concern over Ishigaki becoming a target in a war should the GSDF deploy to the island.[108]

Despite base opposition being an issue in the March 2018 mayoral election, incumbent—and base supporter—Nakayama won the election.[109] In July, he signaled his approval of the GSDF base. Local residents opposed. A civic group on the island collected signatures of more than one-third of eligible voters calling for a public referendum on the new base. According to Ishigaki City's Fundamental Autonomy Ordinance that was enacted in 2010, the mayor is required to hold a referendum on important issues concerning city administration in response to a submission that contains more than one-quarter of the island's eligible voters, which the civic group had obtained. And yet, even after the group submitted their referendum request

---

"Country Officially Sounds Out GSDF Deployment on Ishigaki, Over 500 People to Hirae Ōmata" ["国、石垣に陸自配備正式打診　平得大俣に５００人超"], *Ryūkyū Shimpō*, November 27, 2015.

[106] "200 People Say 'No' to SDF Deployment, Encircle Ishigaki City Hall" ["自衛隊配備に「ノー」２００人、石垣市役所包囲"], *Ryūkyū Shimpō*, June 14, 2016; "Resolution on GSDF Deployment Is 'Tyranny,' Gathering of Residents on Ishigaki Criticize City Assembly" ["陸自配備決議は「横暴」　石垣で集会　市民ら市議会批判"], *Ryūkyū Shimpō*, September 30, 2016; "Ishigaki GSDF Deployment, 800 People Protest, Gathering to Denounce Mayor's Acceptance" ["石垣陸自配備、８００人抗議集会　市長の受け入れ糾弾"], *Ryūkyū Shimpō*, January 30, 2017; "400 People Vigorously Say 'No' to GSDF Deployment, Resident Gathering on Ishigaki" ["陸自配備「ＮＯ」４００人が気勢　石垣島で市民集会"], *Ryūkyū Shimpō*, January 19, 2018.

[107] Although the 70 percent cannot be verified, the fact remains that a substantial number of signatures were collected. See "70% of Ishigaki Residents Sign Petition Opposing SDF Deployment," *Japan Press Weekly*, June 1, 2017.

[108] "Ishigaki Residents' Rally of 400 Says Fervent 'NO' to GSDF Deployment on Ishigaki Island," *Ryūkyū Shimpō*, January 19, 2018.

[109] "Missile Units to Be Deployed on Ishigakijima Island," *Strait Times*, August 3, 2021.

to the city assembly in December 2018, the city assembly voted down the petition, supported by the mayor, citing that the signatures collected were invalid, thereby prompting the group in late 2019 to file a lawsuit against the city government for violating the ordinance.[110] That lawsuit failed, however, because the Naha District Court rejected all the plaintiffs' claims as illegitimate.[111] The plaintiffs appealed, but that too failed in March 2021.[112] The plaintiffs plan to appeal again.

In a separate attempt to block the referendum and strike a blow to those residents who opposed the GSDF base, in December 2019, Ishigaki's city assembly voted on a proposal to abolish the ordinance—and thereby release the mayor of his duty to hold a referendum. The effort ultimately failed by one vote, due to citizen opposition.[113] A few years later, the assembly tried to pass the proposal again, and this time it passed, deleting the provisions on petitioning for a referendum in this ordinance.[114]

As these efforts played out, construction of the base moved forward slowly with relatively no changes to the initial plan. And in February 2022, Nakayama won reelection despite maintaining his approval for the GSDF base and the fact that the central issue in the election was the GSDF deployment.[115]

---

[110] "Ishigaki Islanders Seek Referendum on Deployment of GSDF Missile Base," *Japan Press Weekly*, September 20, 2019; Shogo Mitsuzumi and Daizo Teramoto, "Ishigaki Bylaw Revised in Apparent Bid to Block Referendum," *Asahi Shimbun*, June 29, 2021.

[111] "Naha District Court Dismisses Lawsuit for Referendum about GSDF Deployment to Ishigaki City," trans. by T&CT and Erin Jones, *Ryūkyū Shimpō*, August 27, 2020.

[112] Okada Shōhei, "Public Referendum on GSDF Deployment in Ishigaki, Okinawa, Court Does Not Approve Yet Again" ["沖縄・石垣の陸自配備めぐる住民投票　二審も認めず"], *Asahi Shimbun*, March 23, 2021.

[113] "LDP's Attempt to Block Local Referendum over SDF Base Construction in Ishigaki City Foiled," *Japan Press Weekly*, December 17, 2019.

[114] Mitsuzumi and Teramoto, 2021.

[115] Shogo Mitsuzumi, "All Okinawa's Political Fall in Spotlight After Ishigaki Election," *Asahi Shimbun*, February 28, 2022.

Opposition Gearing Up, Its Effect Still Unknown: Mageshima (Bilateral)

Another relevant example, and one which was still unfolding as of March 2023, involves an effort by both the United States and Japan to establish a new facility on the uninhabited island of Mageshima. Although this effort is still very much in its early phase, there is already evidence to suggest that the two governments will experience the type of opposition seen on Ishigaki and Miyako.

In 2011, the United States and Japan agreed on a plan to move the field carrier landing practice (FCLP) for U.S. carrier–based aircraft from Iwō Jima (Iwō Tō) to Mageshima.[116] The move was prompted largely by the runway on Iwō Jima closing regularly due to poor weather conditions, necessitating these training sessions to shift to other parts of Japan.[117] Because of the noise, however, these training activities are often heavily criticized by local residents. Looking for a permanent location closer to bases on mainland Japan, Mageshima became the leading candidate because it is uninhabited and separated by water from the closest inhabited area. To move forward with its plans, the central government had to purchase the island, thereby necessitating the public release of its plans. This requirement gave opposing forces an opportunity to begin their efforts early.

Despite being uninhabited, Mageshima is under the jurisdiction of the city of Nishinoomote on the island of Tanegashima, about 12 km east of Mageshima. During the 2017 mayoral election, Yaita Shunsuke ran on a platform of opposing Tōkyō's plan and won.[118] This did not stop the central government's plans regarding Mageshima. In November 2019, Tōkyō reached an agreement over its purchase with its owner, followed in December by the MOD notifying the city of Nishinoomote of its intention to establish a base

---

[116] Security Consultative Committee, "Progress on the Realignment of U.S. Forces in Japan," Ministry of Foreign Affairs, Government of Japan, June 21, 2011.

[117] Noriaki Kinoshita and In Tanaka, "Gov't Close to Buying Southern Island for U.S. Carrier Aircraft Landing Practice," *The Mainichi*, November 29, 2018.

[118] Yoshitaka Ito, "Mayor Holding Out on Plan to Use Island for U.S. Military Drills," *Asahi Shimbun*, January 17, 2020a.

there.[119] With efforts moving forward, Yaita continued to oppose the central government's efforts. And in October 2020, he expressed his city's official opposition to the base, citing concerns over potential noise, environmental pollution, and the potential that the base could become a target of an attack, which could threaten the safety of the area.[120] He also noted that the MOD failed to provide clear answers regarding his city's questions about the impact of the noise of aircraft during exercises and the amount of grants to be provided to the city for hosting the training site.[121]

His reasoning reflected the concerns of the residents on the island. Those who opposed cited reasons seen in several of the cases previously examined. One is noise. Even though Mageshima is uninhabited, it sits just 12 km west of Tanegashima. Those who live on Tanegashima who oppose the plan are fearful of noise disturbing them. This is a sensitive topic, given that Kagoshima prefecture has seen a steady increase in the number of low-flying aircraft in recent years, most of which are U.S. military aircraft.[122] Another concern relates to the expected influx of people that would come to Tanegashima. It is expected that with the construction of facilities on Mageshima, lodging for several hundred SDF personnel would be needed in the cities of Nishinoomote or central Tanegashima town, as well as lodging for a dozen or so people in South Tanegashima town for people to service vehicles.[123] Because the island is small, some residents fear that the influx would be too much for the island. Some of those who oppose this plan have

---

[119] Yoshitaka Ito and Ryo Aibara, "Japan Finally Buys Remote Isle for Defense Training Drills," *Asahi Shimbun*, November 30, 2019; Ito, 2020a.

[120] "Local Leader Opposes SDF Base Plan on Kagoshima Isle," Nippon.com, October 7, 2020.

[121] Satoshi Okumura, "New Training Site for U.S. Military Aircraft Opposed by Local Mayor," *Asahi Shimbun*, October 8, 2020.

[122] "102 Cases of Witnessed Low-Flying Aircraft, Are the Majority U.S. Military Aircraft? Lots of Findings on Osprey Propeller Aircraft from Last Year April to December in Kagoshima Prefecture" ["多くは米軍機か、低空飛行目撃102件　鹿児島県内・昨年4～12月　オスプレイ、プロペラ機の情報多数"], *Minami Nippon Shimbun*, January 6, 2022.

[123] Narisawa Kaigo, "MOD Exploring Subsidies for the Mageshima Base Plan, Explanation Expected as Early as Next Week" ["馬毛島基地計画で交付金を検討　防衛省、来週にも説明へ"], *Asahi Shimbun*, December 15, 2021.

also organized a citizen's group called the Liaison of Citizens and Associations that Oppose U.S. Military Facilities on Mageshima (馬毛島への米軍施設に反対する市民団体連絡会), a group that supported the mayor in his January 2021 reelection bid because he too opposed the plan. The group opposes using the island for FCLP training and has collected signatures opposing the establishment of facilities toward that end.[124]

Despite the opposition, the central government pushed forward with critical elements of the plan from late 2021. First, in December, the Kishida Fumio administration approved a draft budget for FY 2022 with 318.3 billion yen ($2.8 billion) earmarked for the plan.[125] Then, in a January 2022 joint statement from U.S. and Japanese officials, Mageshima is explicitly referenced, noting that "the United States welcomed Japan's decision in its [Japanese Fiscal Year] 2022 draft budget to fund construction of the Mageshima facility consistent with the 2011 SCC [Security Consultative Committee] document."[126] Following that, Mayor Yaita and the Nishinoomote municipal government held discussions with 51 local organizations, including the Chamber of Commerce, to exchange opinions on the issue. While there were voices of opposition, there were also calls to the mayor to hold discussions with the central government about how to protect the safety of the local residents, as well as expectations regarding grants given to the town by Tōkyō for agreeing to establish the facility.[127] Then, later the same month, it was reported that the central government had announced 13 bid-

---

[124] "'Toward the Repeal of the Mageshima Base Plan,' Opposing Resident Group of Nishinoomote Submits 24,000 Signatures to the MOD" ["馬毛島基地計画の撤回を」西之表の市民団体が反対署名2万4000筆を防衛省に提出"], Yahoo Japan, February 5, 2022.

[125] Matsuyama Naoki, "FY22 Draft Budget, Defense Expenses at Record High, Will Reach 6 Trillion Yen Range for the First Time with Supplemental Included?" ["22年度当初予算、防衛費が過去最大に　補正込みでは初の6兆円台"], Asahi Shimbun, December 24, 2021.

[126] U.S. Department of State, "Joint Statement of the U.S.-Japan Security Consultative Committee ('2+2')," January 6, 2022.

[127] Gushiken Sunao, "'Disapproval' Has Disappeared from the Mouth of the Local Mayor on the Mageshima Base Plan" ["馬毛島の基地整備計画、地元市長の口から消えた「不同意」"], Asahi Shimbun, February 3, 2021.

ding contracts for projects related to the facilities, such as a control tower and fuel depot.[128]

With the central government making progress in its plans and local associations appearing to soften in their opposition, despite his public opposition to the plan (including winning reelection on a platform of his opposition), in early February 2022, Yaita appeared to have changed his ardent opposition of the plan toward one more open to considering it.[129] In a meeting with then–Defense Minister Kishi Nobuo, rather than repeating his past opposition, Yaita called for creating a forum between the municipal and central governments to discuss the issue on the assumption that the FCLP training exercises would be moved to Mageshima and that a new SDF base would be built; he also requested "special consideration" of tax subsidies distributed to local governments that agree to cooperate with efforts to relocate U.S. military facilities and drills.[130] While not explicitly saying that he supported the plan, his requests demonstrated that his government was prepared to accept the central government's plan. Importantly, and something to watch in the months and years ahead, Shiota Kōichi, the governor of Kagoshima prefecture (of which Tanegashima is a part), has made it very clear to MOD officials that he is not comfortable with the pace of progress given that he has stated that local citizens have not had sufficient explana-

---

[128] "Mageshima SDF Base Plan, the MOD Places Order for Construction Amidst Environment Assessment, Kagoshima Prefecture 'Hard to Comprehend'" ["馬毛島自衛隊基地計画　防衛省、環境アセス途中で本体工事発注　鹿児島県「理解しかねる"], *Minami Nippon Shimbun*, January 27, 2022.

[129] "'Objection' of Nishinoomote City Mayor Fading to Mageshima Base Plan, 'Concerns About Consent or Lack of Consent Fostering Divisions Among Residents'" ["馬毛島基地計画　西之表市長から消えた「不同意」「同意の可否、市民の分断助長する心配がある"], *Minami Nippon Shimbun*, February 5, 2022.

[130] Gushiken Sunao and Narisawa Kaigo, "Mayor Tones Down Opposition to U.S. Military Drills on Island," *Asahi Shimbun*, February 4, 2022.

tion of the MOD's process.[131] And opposition groups continue their efforts to oppose the plan.[132]

Whether the existing opposition, by local groups or the government of Kagoshima prefecture, will result in any changes to the plan remains to be seen. The outcome is particularly uncertain because in addition to Yaita's reversal not all Tanegashima residents oppose the plan. Similar to the case of Yonaguni, some express the hope that economic benefits could follow from an increase in SDF personnel on the island through greater consumption and the development of island infrastructure.[133] At present, however, the Mageshima plan appears to be moving forward with no changes or delays caused by local opposition. In the January 2023 joint statement of U.S. and Japanese officials, "progress and future prospects for the development of the SDF facility on Mageshima" is explicitly welcomed, indicating the alliance's ongoing commitment to the new base.[134]

---

[131] "Kagoshima, Prefectural Governor Says 'I Don't Know the Process' on Mageshima SDF Base Construction" ["鹿児島 馬毛島の自衛隊基地建設 県知事 'プロセス分からない'"], NHK, January 13, 2022.

[132] David McElhinney, "Opposition Increasing for New U.S. Training Site on Mageshima," *Tokyo Weekender*, April 16, 2021.

[133] Gushiken Sunao and Shinichi Fujiwara, "Mageshima Swayed by National Policy, What They Saw at the Location They Accepted After a Lot of Turmoil" ["国策にゆれる馬毛島混乱経て受け入れた先行地で見えてきたものは"], *Asahi Shimbun*, October 27, 2021.

[134] U.S. Mission Japan, "Joint Statement of the Security Consultative Committee (2+2)," January 11, 2023.

CHAPTER 3

Conclusion

Key Takeaways

None of the cases examined in the preceding chapter preordain Japan's response to the introduction of any new defense capabilities in Japan. Or suggest the inevitability of Japan's response. While the cases (summarized in Table 3.1) are few in number and widely different in nature, they nevertheless provide several useful insights that DoD and DoS should consider if Washington seeks to deploy new defense capabilities in Japan in the years ahead:

- **Location matters.** Although the cases show that opposition to either U.S. or Japanese presence can occur at any location in Japan, opposition to new U.S. military presence is likely to be stronger on the island of Okinawa than in other locations. Introducing new U.S. capabilities—

TABLE 3.1
Summary of Cases

Result	Type of Access Sought
Successful implementation	• Patriot storage facility inside Kadena Air Force Base • AN/TPY-2 radar systems in SDF base at Kyōgasaki • MQ-9 Reaper in SDF Kanoya Air Base • Surveillance unit at SDF base on Yonaguni • GSDF base on Ishigaki
Partial implementation	• SDF base on Miyako
Stalled implementation	• FRF at Henoko • SDF Ospreys at Saga Airport • FCLP on Mageshima (possibly too soon to tell)
Cancelation	• Aegis Ashore systems at two GSDF bases

and personnel—would go against decades of trying to reduce U.S. presence there. This does not mean that deploying new capabilities would be impossible, but the United States should expect implementation to possibly take a long time, motivate resident opposition, and likely encounter several legal challenges along the way. Importantly, while the resentment of many people in Okinawa regarding what some call the "burden" that the island has to bear for hosting U.S. bases and personnel forms the basis for much opposition in Okinawa (and has played a key role in delaying the construction of the FRF), the intensity of local resistance appears to differ between the island of Okinawa and other islands in Okinawa prefecture (e.g., Yonaguni, Miyako, and Ishigaki). As shown in Chapter 2, there is some indication of less widespread and intense opposition to defense deployments in these outer islands compared with the island of Okinawa itself.

- **Capability type may matter.** Sensitivity to new capabilities appears to be more intense when a hosting community perceives that doing so will result in making the community a target of attack or somehow present a threat to residents. We saw this demonstrated in opposition voiced against Aegis Ashore, the MQ-9 Reaper, and the new SDF bases on the Nansei Shotō. Sensitivities also appear to increase when a new capability is noisy or capable of accidents that can harm residents. Such perceived threats have partly driven the opposition to Futenma, the introduction of the GSDF's V-22 Ospreys, and the construction of facilities on Mageshima. Introducing nonkinetic capabilities, by contrast, appears less likely to spark opposition, particularly if they are not large, visible platforms that may cause noise or accidents. It is possible this accounts for the lack of opposition to the Patriot missile facility on Kadena Air Base, the new base on Yonaguni, and the eventual acquiescence to the temporary deployment of the MQ-9 Reaper.
- **Central government agreement is a necessary but not sufficient condition.** The Japanese central government is the most important actor for deciding whether to approve a U.S. or MOD/SDF request for a new capability or facility. Yet, its approval alone is not sufficient to ensure implementation because it is the responsibility of the central government to address the concerns of local host communities. And discussions and negotiations between the central and local govern-

ments provide opportunities for opposition forces to exert influence. Either through formal approvals related to construction, public referendums, or lawsuits, these local actors have used legal, administrative, and bureaucratic means by which to prevent or delay implementation of a central government plan. Although central government authority trumps any local government decision, Tōkyō has historically proven reluctant to force its way on matters regarding the presence of armed forces, U.S. or Japanese. Therefore, although Tōkyō's decision will always be final, implementing that decision against a committed opposition could take time and, in the course of implementation, lead to changes in the initial plan.

- **Size of the capability may matter.** Although evidence suggests less opposition against nonkinetic capabilities, it could be the case that the lack of a sizable opposition may be a function of the visibility of the capability. Unlike the deployment of tiltrotor aircraft or missile batteries, small, virtually invisible changes to presence—such as the addition of the Patriot missile facility—likely go unnoticed by the public. It is possible that small, nonvisible additions will not generate public opposition or provide a lightning rod around which opposition forces can rally, particularly if no environment assessments or large-scale construction are needed. Large-scale, visible changes, particularly those that require environmental assessments or large-scale construction and basing, will help mobilize local opposition.

- **Whether a capability requires a new base or can be deployed to an existing base may not matter.** As the munition storage for Patriot missiles at Kadena Air Base demonstrates, it appears to be easier to deploy new capabilities inside a U.S. military base, particularly if that capability is nonkinetic and not highly visible. Although not examined in this report, the Marine Corps' deployment of its Osprey tiltrotor aircraft to U.S. bases in Japan appears to have occurred relatively according to plan, despite some initial opposition. Such cases suggest that it is possible that deployments taking place inside a U.S. facility could matter for successful implementation. While logically it would make sense that introducing new capabilities onto existing U.S. or SDF bases would be easier than constructing new bases, the Nansei Shotō and Mageshima cases show that Tōkyō can proceed with construction of new facilities against a committed local opposition. And the Aegis Ashore case shows that deploying a new capability to an existing SDF base is not a guarantee of success. This finding suggests that the difficulty of constructing a new base or new facilities may not be a constraining factor. That said, the FRF example suggests that a committed opposition—especially by local government officials—can dramatically stall efforts that require new construction and the associated administrative approvals by prefectural authorities. Collectively, it is hard to draw a conclusion on whether the need for a new base or use of an existing base matters.

- **Level of local opposition appears to depend on how directly the local communities view the capability as affecting the peace, safety, and security of the community.** While location, visibility, and capability type appear to all play some role in motivating opposition, local communities' opposition to any U.S. or SDF posture change tends to revolve around whether that change will have adverse effects on residents, their lifestyle, and their livelihoods. Fears of becoming a target, for example, were prevalent in most of the cases examined. So too were concerns about off-base incidents and accidents caused by the expected personnel influx. Even when the capability was nonkinetic, communities were motivated to oppose posture changes that could result in adverse health effects, such as electromagnetic interference or noise.

Recommendations

Although the case studies examined in this report do not represent all experiences of introducing new defense capabilities in Japan, they do offer insights into recent examples. Drawing on the takeaways above, this report closes with five broad recommendations that the U.S. government should consider when pursuing new capabilities in Japan.

- **Support the domestic process.** Local communities want their concerns to be heard. Because of the political difficulties that the central government faces from some local base-hosting communities, Tōkyō needs to pursue dialogue internally with its local leaders and communities through meetings, forums, information exchanges, and other engagement mechanisms. This process is bound to take time and not progress in a linear manner. Yet, letting this process play out and supporting Tōkyō in its endeavors with any necessary information will be appreciated by Tōkyō. Comparing the differences of the FRF and Mageshima cases appears to show where extended dialogue could pay dividends. Yaita initially opposed the Mageshima plan, despite the island being uninhabited, which reflected the concerns of nearby residents about the impact of the FCLP on their daily lives. Yaita's opposition appeared to soften after the forum between the municipal and central governments. This forum was missing in the FRF case in Okinawa, and three decades later, that situation is not yet resolved. Holding such formal consultations between local or municipal and central governments is, therefore, critical and should be incorporated into U.S. planning initiatives as a necessary step to get effective and sustainable collaboration with allies.

- **Maintain transparency and open communication.** While Tōkyō will take the lead on interfacing with local communities, there will be many requests for information. Not all new force posture initiatives will elicit opposition, but it can be safely assumed that anything that flies, fires, or emits sounds or smells that communities could find disturbing is going to face complaints. Therefore, it is imperative for Tōkyō to maintain dialogue with local communities and answer their concerns with timely information to ensure the sustainability of U.S. presence. Toward this end, the more that the United States can do to provide full transparency of the intended unit size, impact on communities, and mitigation measures to potential concerns, the easier it will be for Tōkyō to engage its local communities in an informed manner.

- **Use routine exercises to normalize new types of capabilities or presence.** Because acceptance levels of U.S. forces vary in different parts of Japan, there is bound to be varied responses to the introduction of new capabilities or force presence in different parts of the country. Although not guaranteed to elicit acquiescence by local communities, routine exercises are one way that the U.S. military could help gain better acceptance of a new capability or force posture. By bringing in a desired capability or presence into a community for a short amount of time on a routine basis, the U.S. military can gauge local community response, hear potential concerns about that capability, and over time, pursue mitigation measures to address their concerns. Importantly, such exercises also present an important opportunity for relationship-building between U.S. forces and the community, which helps build trust. It is possible—but not guaranteed—that over time the routine presence of the capability could become normalized to the point that opposition is minimized.

- **Address local community concerns where possible.** While not every concern raised by a local community can be adequately addressed to the point of obtaining support, there are areas where the United States can demonstrate its sincere intent to work with the community and thereby obtain a more sustainable presence. For example, the U.S. Army's application of noise-reducing mufflers to the AN/TPY-2 equipment appeared to address local concerns, dispelling opposition. Similarly, Japanese central government officials' explicit statements about the MQ-9 Reapers being strictly limited to surveillance operations and not carrying weapons appeared to disarm local opposition. Making such promises or changes are not going to be possible in all cases, but where possible, the U.S. military may find more success in implementing their plans.
- **Pick your battles.** Not every community will openly welcome an increased U.S. military presence. By the same token, not every community will oppose. Some capabilities, such as kinetic ones, are likely to elicit more opposition than others in some communities. Being more mindful of local sentiment can help the United States craft smarter requests.

Closing

The U.S. armed forces cannot assume that requests for deploying new capabilities in Japan will proceed smoothly or as planned. This is likely to be the case anywhere in Japan, but particularly in Okinawa prefecture. In this prefecture, where the issue of U.S. military presence is predominantly concentrated in this small area of land, and the governments of both Japan and the

United States have been striving to make the U.S. military presence more sustainable, requesting a new U.S. footprint likely would be met with opposition by local leaders and some segment of the resident population. After all, despite pro-U.S. sentiment, the anti-base movement "remains strong and vocal in Okinawa," driven largely by concerns that U.S. presence degrades the local quality of life with regard to personal safety, noise, crime, and the natural environment, as well as the lingering elements of pacifism and anti-militarism.[1] That said, introducing nonkinetic capabilities could likely face a relatively smaller challenge compared with the kinetic assets.

Regardless of what is requested, the cases examined in this report highlight the critical importance of remembering that although Japan's central government has the authority to make decisions regarding the country's defenses, without local buy-in by the communities asked to host these capabilities, such decisions can cause fear and anger among local governments and communities which, in turn, could lead to numerous challenges in implementing the plan. The worst result, and one that the case of Okinawa highlights, is that if Washington and Tōkyō forge ahead with a plan that does not have the understanding of the local people, "the furious opposition could well direct itself towards the U.S. forces and make the stable operation of other bases in Okinawa, including Kadena Air Base, difficult."[2]

---

[1] Chanlett-Avery and Rinehart, 2016, p. 7.

[2] Tamaki, undated.

Abbreviations

AN/TPY-2	Army/Navy Transportable Radar Surveillance system
ASDF	Air Self-Defense Force
BMD	ballistic missile defense
DoD	U.S. Department of Defense
DoS	U.S. Department of State
DPRI	Defense Policy Review Initiative
FCLP	field carrier landing practice
FRF	Futenma Replacement Facility
FY	fiscal year
GSDF	Ground Self-Defense Force
MEF	Marine Expeditionary Force
MOD	Ministry of Defense
SACO	Special Action Committee on Okinawa
SDF	Self-Defense Forces

References

"102 Cases of Witnessed Low-Flying Aircraft, Are the Majority U.S. Military Aircraft? Lots of Findings on Osprey Propeller Aircraft from Last Year April to December in Kagoshima Prefecture" ["多くは米軍機か、低空飛行目撃102件 鹿児島県内 昨年4～12月オスプレイ、プロペラ機の情報多数"], *Minami Nippon Shimbun*, January 6, 2022. As of October 14, 2022: https://373news.com/_news/storyid/149327/? fbclid=IwAR2d1Y_9M FwdrMdnK3z4kBsvYUT3uwMXGtzh6P0Q8yVU3L44JwROUdEuTRk

"130 Residents Protest the Start of Construction, 'No' to the GSDF Deployment to Miyako" ["宮古島陸自配備にノー 市民１３０人、着工に抗議"], *Ryūkyū Shimpō*, December 14, 2017. As of March 3, 2022: https://ryukyushimpo.jp/news/entry-630570.html

"200 People Say 'No' to SDF Deployment, Encircle Ishigaki City Hall" ["自衛 隊配備に「ノー」２００人、石垣市役所包囲"], *Ryūkyū Shimpō*, June 14, 2016. As of March 3, 2022: https://ryukyushimpo.jp/news/entry-297464.html

"400 People Vigorously Say 'No' to GSDF Deployment, Resident Gathering on Ishigaki" ["陸自配備「NO」４００人が気勢石垣島で市民集会"], *Ryūkyū Shimpō*, January 19, 2018. As of February 24, 2022: https://ryukyushimpo.jp/news/entry-648909.html

"70% of Ishigaki Residents Sign Petition Opposing SDF Deployment," *Japan Press Weekly*, June 1, 2017.

"About Information Relating to Aegis Ashore" ["イージス アショアに関する情 報について"], Akita City, undated.

"About the Resolution Regarding Opposition to the Deployment Plan to the GSDF's Araya Training Area of the Ground-Deployed Aegis System (Aegis Ashore) Which Threatens the Safety of Residents" ["住民の安全を脅かす陸上 配備型イージス システム（イージス アショア）の 陸上自衛隊新屋演習場への 配備計画反対に関する決議について"], Akita City, June 3, 2019.

Akiyama, Shinichi, "GSDF to Delay Shipment of Ospreys to Japan as Local Opposition Mounts," *The Mainichi*, September 24, 2018.

Andrews, Daniel, "New Patriot Missile Storage Facility Unveiled in Okinawa," U.S. Army, May 24, 2021.

"Base Concentration Is 'Unequal' in Okinawa Prefecture (61%), Different from 40% Nationwide, Shimpo/Mainichi Public Poll" ["基地集中は「不平等」沖縄 県内61％全国40％と落差新報 毎日世論調査"], *Ryūkyū Shimpo*, May 10, 2022.

Cabinet Office, "Government Plan Concerning the Relocation of Futenma Airfield" ["普天間飛行場の移設に係る政府方針"], Government of Japan, cabinet decision December 28, 1999, abolition May 30, 2006.

Cabinet Secretariat, *National Security Strategy of Japan*, Government of Japan, December 16, 2022. As of January 27, 2023:
https://www.cas.go.jp/jp/siryou/221216anzenhoshou/nss-e.pdf

Chanlett-Avery, Emma, and Ian E. Rinehart, *The U.S. Military Presence in Okinawa and the Futenma Base Controversy*, Congressional Research Service, R42645, January 20, 2016.

"Chronicles of the Relocation Problem (by Year)" ["移設問題の動向 (年表)"], Nago City, undated.

"Contents of the Last Meeting, Mr. Hashimoto and Mr. Ota's 'Honeymoon,' Governor Looks Away as Prime Minister Pressures, 'It Was a Bizarre Atmosphere That Froze the Place'" ["その場が凍り付く異様な雰囲気だった」迫る首相にうつむく知事　「蜜月」の橋本・大田氏、最後の会談の中身"], *Okinawa Times*, March 13, 2022.

"Country Officially Sounds Out GSDF Deployment on Ishigaki, Over 500 People to Hirae Ōmata" ["国、石垣に陸自配備正式打診　平得大俣に５００人超"], *Ryūkyū Shimpō*, November 27, 2015.

"Defense Political Vice Minister Suggests Ammunition Depot in Bora Mine to Mayor Shimoji" ["保良鉱山に弾薬庫　防衛政務官が下地市長に打診"], *Ryūkyū Shimpō*, January 17, 2018.

"Distrust Between Central Gov't, Okinawa Pref. Lingers Ahead of Court Talks on Futenma," *The Mainichi*, March 22, 2016.

DoD—*See* U.S. Department of Defense.

DoS—*See* U.S. Department of State.

Duncan, Bryan, "Army Signaleers Keep 14th Missile Defense Battery Connected," *PACOM News*, August 26, 2015. As of March 11, 2022:
https://www.pacom.mil/Media/News/Article/614918/
army-signaleers-keep-14th-missile-defense-battery-connected/

Eckstein, Megan, "Japan Officially Ends Aegis Ashore Plans After National Security Council Deliberations," *USNI News*, June 26, 2020. As of March 21, 2022:
https://news.usni.org/2020/06/26/japan-officially-ends-aegis-ashore-plans-after-national-security-council-deliberations

"Ex-Mayor Held in Bribery Case Tied to GSDF Camp on Okinawa Isle," *Asahi Shimbun*, May 13, 2021. As of October 11, 2022:
https://www.asahi.com/ajw/articles/14347695

Fackler, Martin, "90,000 Protest U.S. Base on Okinawa," *New York Times*, April 25, 2010. As of October 11, 2022:
https://www.nytimes.com/2010/04/26/world/asia/26okinawa.html

"Formation of Miyako Garrison Complete, GSDF 700 Person in Scale, Even Though Request Made to Postpone Due to COVID Measures, Ceremony Proceeded" ["宮古駐屯地の編成完了　陸自、７００人規模　コロナ防止で延期要請も式典強行"], *Ryūkyū Shimpō*, April 5, 2020. As of March 3, 2022:
https://ryukyushimpo.jp/news/entry-1102331.html

Fujiwara, Shinichi, "Clumsy Strategy Weakening Bid to Shore Up Remote Island Defenses," *Asahi Shimbun*, April 29, 2020. As of March 3, 2022:
https://www.asahi.com/ajw/articles/13300444

"Gov't Uses Power of Money to Have Residents Accept U.S. Radar Base Construction," *Japan Press Weekly*, May 11, 2014. As of March 15, 2022:
https://www.japan-press.co.jp/modules/news/index.php?id=7179

"GSDF Ospreys Rejected by Saga Get 5-Year OK to Deploy in Chiba," *Asahi Shimbun*, December 25, 2019. As of February 25, 2022:
https://www.asahi.com/ajw/articles/13055974

"GSDF to Deploy Ospreys to Chiba as Fishermen in Saga Block Move," *Asahi Shimbun*, May 15, 2019. As of March 2, 2022:
https://www.asahi.com/ajw/articles/13063679

"GSDF's Deployment of Ospreys to Saga Airport Likely Faces Delay," *The Mainichi*, July 19, 2017.

Gushiken Sunao, "'Disapproval' Has Disappeared from the Mouth of the Local Mayor on the Mageshima Base Plan" ["馬毛島の基地整備計画、地元市長の口から消えた「不同意」"], *Asahi Shimbun*, February 3, 2021. As of October 14, 2022:
https://www.asahi.com/articles/ASQ236RPXQ23TIPE01V.html

Gushiken Sunao and Narisawa Kaigo, "Mayor Tones Down Opposition to U.S. Military Drills on Island," *Asahi Shimbun*, February 4, 2022. As of October 12, 2022:
https://www.asahi.com/ajw/articles/14540345

Gushiken Sunao and Shinichi Fujiwara, "Mageshima Swayed by National Policy, What They Saw at the Location They Accepted After a Lot of Turmoil" ["国策にゆれる馬毛島　混乱経て受け入れた先行地で見えてきたものは"], *Asahi Shimbun*, October 27, 2021. As of October 14, 2022:
https://www.asahi.com/articles/ASPBV4RL3PBQTIPE01G.html?iref=pc_rellink_03

Handa Shigeru, "Aegis Ashore, Big Contradiction in 'Review in Akita, Going as Planned in Yamaguchi'" ["イージス　アショア「秋田で見直し、山口は計画通り」の大きな矛盾"], *Gendai Business*, May 9, 2020. As of March 21, 2022:
https://gendai.ismedia.jp/articles/-/72417?imp=0

Hara, Shogo, "GSDF's Radars on China on Japan's Westmost Island Less Divisive 5 Years After Deployment," *Japan News*, March 28, 2021.

Hayashi Kunihiro, "At the Town Meeting in Abu Town, Voices of Opposition to the Ground Aegis Deployment" ["陸上イージス配備に反発の声　阿武町で住民説明会"], *Asahi Shimbun*, December 21, 2019. As of March 21, 2022: https://www.asahi.com/articles/ASMDN4DYTMDNTZNB00W.html

Hornung, Jeffrey W., "Japan Is Canceling a U.S. Missile Defense System," *Foreign Policy*, July 2, 2020. As of March 21, 2022: https://foreignpolicy.com/2020/07/02/japan-aegis-ashore-expense-cancel-united-states-alliance/

"Information Regarding the Temporary Deployment of U.S. Military Unmanned MQ-9 Aircraft" ["米軍無人機MQ-9の一時展開に関する情報について"], Kanoya City, October 11, 2022. As of October 11, 2022: https://www.city.kanoya.lg.jp/suishin/mq9.html

Ishibashi, Otohide, "Statement by Chairman Opposing the Deployment of Aegis Ashore in Araya Training Area" ["新屋演習場へのイージス・アショア配備に反対する会長声明"], Tohoku Federation of Bar Associations, July 12, 2019. As of March 21, 2022: https://www.t-benren.org/statement/261

"Ishigaki GSDF Deployment, 800 People Protest, Gathering to Denounce Mayor's Acceptance" ["石垣陸自配備、８００人抗議集会　市長の受け入れ糾弾"], *Ryūkyū Shimpō*, January 30, 2017. As of March 2, 2022: https://ryukyushimpo.jp/news/entry-435659.html

"Ishigaki Islanders Seek Referendum on Deployment of GSDF Missile Base," *Japan Press Weekly*, September 20, 2019. As of February 24, 2022: https://www.japan-press.co.jp/modules/news/index.php?id=12446

"Ishigaki Residents' Rally of 400 Says Fervent 'NO' to GSDF Deployment on Ishigaki Island," *Ryūkyū Shimpō*, January 19, 2018. As of October 11, 2022: http://english.ryukyushimpo.jp/2018/01/25/28343/

Ishino, Harumi, "Opposing U.S. 'Missile Offense' Radar Base in Kyoto," *Space4Peace* blog, March 26, 2015. As of March 15, 2022: http://space4peace.blogspot.com/2015/03/opposing-us-missile-offense-radar-base.html

Ito, Yoshitaka, "Mayor Holding Out on Plan to Use Island for U.S. Military Drills," *Asahi Shimbun*, January 17, 2020a. As of October 12, 2022: https://www.asahi.com/ajw/articles/13042846

Ito, Yoshitaka, "SDF's 1st Osprey Force Deployed 'Temporarily' for 5 Years in Chiba," *Asahi Shimbun*, March 27, 2020b. As of February 25, 2022: https://www.asahi.com/ajw/articles/13250279

Ito, Yoshitaka, and Ryo Aibara, "Japan Finally Buys Remote Isle for Defense Training Drills," *Asahi Shimbun*, November 30, 2019. As of October 12, 2022: https://www.asahi.com/ajw/articles/13058266

Jameson, Sam, "Huge Rally in Okinawa Denounces U.S. Bases," *Los Angeles Times*, October 22, 1995.

"Japan City Opposes Plan to Deploy Military Drones to Local Base," *Financial Assets*, February 5, 2022. As of February 11, 2022: https://fa.news/articles/ japan_city_opposes_plan_to_deploy_military_drones_to_local_base-117662/

"Japan Defense Ministry to Deploy Osprey Aircraft to Chiba Pref. Base," *The Mainichi*, March 27, 2018. As of March 17, 2022: https://mainichi.jp/english/articles/20180327/p2a/00m/0na/015000c

"Japan Halts Deployment of U.S.-Made Missile Defense System," Kyodo News, June 16, 2020. As of March 21, 2022: https://english.kyodonews.net/news/2020/06/c4e83631fd00-urgent-japan-to-halt-process-to-deploy-aegis-ashore-missile-defense-system.html

"Japan Officially Takes Delivery of First Bell Boeing Tiltrotor Aircraft V-22 for Japanese Self Defense Force," *Navy Recognition*, July 2020. As of March 17, 2022: https://www.navyrecognition.com/index.php/news/defence-news/2020/ july/8721-japan-officially-takes-delivery-of-first-bell-boeing-tiltrotor-aircraft-v-22-for-japanese-self-defense-force.html

"Japan Scraps Aegis Ashore Deployment Plan in Akita," Nippon.com, May 6, 2020. As of March 21, 2022: https://www.nippon.com/en/news/yjj2020050600381/

"Japan Suspends Aegis Ashore Deployment," Arms Control Association, July/ August 2020. As of April 4, 2022: https://www.armscontrol.org/act/2020-07/news-briefs/ japan-suspends-aegis-ashore-deployment

"Japan to Talk with U.S. Over 180 Bil. Yen Aegis Ashore Deal," Kyodo News, June 16, 2020. As of March 21, 2022: https://english.kyodonews.net/news/2020/06/1ca19580a9c1-land-based-missile-defense-deployment-plan-no-longer-rational-kono.html

"Kagoshima, Prefectural Governor Says 'I Don't Know the Process' on Mageshima SDF Base Construction" ["鹿児島 馬毛島の自衛隊基地建設 県知事 'プロセス分からない'"], NHK, January 13, 2022. As of October 14, 2022: https://www3.nhk.or.jp/news/html/20220113/k10013429261000.html?fbclid=I wAR0MBAqP1BPsYxxuKCygZgtipo4LmITxoFek5tFEvR0PIdqq2uoT5ezZ gaU

Kamiya Nobuharu, "Various Problems Regarding the 12th Henoko Litigation Supreme Court Decision" ["第12回 辺野古訴訟最高裁判決を巡る諸問題"], *LIBRA*, Vol. 17, No. 11, November 2017. As of April 20, 2022:
https://www.toben.or.jp/message/libra/pdf/2017_11/p30-32.pdf

"Kanoya, Voices of Complaint from Residents About the U.S. Military Unmanned Aircraft Deployment" ["鹿屋, 米軍無人機配備巡り住民から不満の声"], Kagoshima Yomiuri Terebi, February 15, 2022. As of March 21, 2022:
https://www.kyt-tv.com/nnn/news104z1qkap30v74dyr12.html

Karako, Tom, "Shield of the Pacific: Japan as a Giant Aegis Destroyer," Center for Strategic and International Studies, May 23, 2018. As of April 4, 2022:
https://www.csis.org/analysis/shield-pacific-japan-giant-aegis-destroyer

Kawaguchi, Shun, "Signature Campaign Opposing Aegis Ashore Missile Defense System Held in North Japan," *The Mainichi*, December 16, 2019. As of March 21, 2022:
https://mainichi.jp/english/articles/20191216/p2a/00m/0na/006000c

Kinoshita, Noriaki, and In Tanaka, "Gov't Close to Buying Southern Island for US Carrier Aircraft Landing Practice," *The Mainichi*, November 29, 2018. As of October 12, 2022:
https://mainichi.jp/english/articles/20181129/p2a/00m/0na/001000c

"Kisarazu Mayor Gives Nod to 'Temporary' Deployment of Ospreys to Local SDF Base," *Japan Press Weekly*, December 26, 2019. As of March 17, 2022:
https://www.japan-press.co.jp/modules/news/index.php?id=12653

"Kyoto Agrees to Let U.S. Install X-Band Radar in Kyotango," *Japan Times*, September 20, 2013. As of March 11, 2022:
https://www.japantimes.co.jp/news/2013/09/20/national/kyoto-agrees-to-let-u-s-install-x-band-radar-in-kyotango/

"Kyoto Residents Organize to Block Installation of U.S. Missile Defense Radar Site," *Japan Press Weekly*, May 24, 2013. As of March 11, 2022:
https://www.japan-press.co.jp/s/news/?id=5713

Lattanzio, Thomas, "Aegis Ashore Cancellation—Impulsive Blunder or Strategic Opportunity?" Stimson Center, July 29, 2020. As of April 4, 2022:
https://www.stimson.org/2020/aegis-ashore-cancellation-impulsive-blunder-or-strategic-opportunity/

"LDP's Attempt to Block Local Referendum over SDF Base Construction in Ishigaki City Foiled," *Japan Press Weekly*, December 17, 2019. As of February 24, 2022:
https://www.japan-press.co.jp/modules/news/?id=12615&pc_flag=ON

"Local Leader Opposes SDF Base Plan on Kagoshima Isle," Nippon.com, October 7, 2020. As of March 2, 2022:
https://www.nippon.com/en/news/yjj2020100700870/

"Local Residents Don't Want US Military Base to Be Built in Kyoto," *Japan Press Weekly*, October 5, 2014. As of March 11, 2022:
https://www.japan-press.co.jp/modules/news/index.php?id=7594

"Local Residents Oppose Construction of GSDF Facility on Miyako from Early Morning, 'Don't Build a Dangerous Ammunition Depot'" ["危険な弾薬庫造るな」宮古島の陸自施設着工 市民、早朝から抗議"], *Ryūkyū Shimpō*, October 8, 2019. As of March 4, 2022:
https://ryukyushimpo.jp/news/entry-1003365.html

"Looking Back at Governors' 'Peace Declarations,' with a Strong Sense of Anti-War and Base Issues" ["歴代知事の「平和宣言」を振り返る 反戦、基地問題思い込め"], *Ryūkyū Shimpō*, June 21, 2019. As of March 10, 2022:
https://ryukyushimpo.jp/news/entry-929073.html

"Mageshima SDF Base Plan, the MOD Places Order for Construction Amidst Environment Assessment, Kagoshima Prefecture 'Hard to Comprehend'" ["馬毛島自衛隊基地計画 防衛省、環境アセス途中で本体工事発注 鹿児島県「理解しかねる"], *Minami Nippon Shimbun*, January 27, 2022. As of March 20, 2022:
https://373news.com/_news/storyid/150494/

Mahnken, Thomas G., Travis Sharp, Billy Fabian, and Peter Kouretsos, *Tightening the Chain: Implementing a Strategy of Maritime Pressure in the Western Pacific*, Center for Strategic and Budgetary Assessments, May 23, 2019. As of January 27, 2023:
https://csbaonline.org/research/publications/
implementing-a-strategy-of-maritime-pressure-in-the-western-pacific

Maib, Charlie, "Kyogamisaki Communications Site: Knife Edge of Freedom," Defense Visual Information Distribution Service, March 7, 2022. As of March 11, 2022:
https://www.dvidshub.net/news/415894/
kyogamisaki-communications-site-knife-edge-freedom

Malyasov, Dylan, "Japan Deploys New V-22 Osprey Aircraft to Chiba Amid Protests," *Defence Blog*, July 10, 2020. As of March 17, 2022:
https://defence-blog.com/
japan-deploys-new-v-22-osprey-aircraft-to-chiba-amid-protests/

Matsuyama, Naoki, "FY22 Draft Budget, Defense Expenses at Record High, Will Reach 6 Trillion Yen Range for the First Time with Supplemental Included" ["22年度当初予算、防衛費が過去最大に 補正込みでは初の6兆円台"], *Asahi Shimbun*, December 24, 2021. As of October 14, 2022:
https://www.asahi.com/articles/ASPDS4CDPPDRUTFK013.html

McCormack, Gavan, "Yonaguni: Dilemmas of a Frontier Island in the East China Sea," *Asia-Pacific Journal*, Vol. 10, Iss. 40, No. 1, September 30, 2012. As of April 4, 2022:
https://apjjf.org/site/make_pdf/3837

McElhinney, David, "Opposition Increasing for New U.S. Training Site on Mageshima," *Tokyo Weekender*, April 16, 2021. As of October 12, 2022:
https://www.tokyoweekender.com/2021/04/the-environmental-costs-of-the-us-airbase-on-mageshima/

Mieno Yasushi, "The System of Lawsuits to Confirm the Illegality of Inaction by the Government Against a Local Government" ["国の自治体に対する不作為の違法確認訴訟制度のあり方"], *Jichi Soken*, Vol. 467, September 2017. As of April 20, 2022:
https://www.jstage.jst.go.jp/article/jichisoken/43/467/43_62/_pdf/-char/ja

Ministry of Defense, "Council on Measures Concerning the Relocation of Futenma Airfield (2nd Session)" ["普天間飛行場の移設に係る措置に関する協議会（第2回）"], Government of Japan, December 25, 2006. As of October 11, 2022:
https://www.mod.go.jp/j/approach/zaibeigun/saihen/kyougikai/061225_op.pdf

Ministry of Defense, "Council on Measures Concerning the Relocation of Futenma Airfield (3rd Session)" ["普天間飛行場の移設に係る措置に関する協議会（第3回）"], Government of Japan, January 19, 2007. As of October 11, 2022:
https://www.mod.go.jp/j/approach/zaibeigun/saihen/kyougikai/070119_op.pdf

Ministry of Defense, "Minister of Defense Press Conference" ["防衛大臣記者会見"], Government of Japan, February 26, 2019. As of October 11, 2022:
https://warp.da.ndl.go.jp/info:ndljp/pid/11623291/www.mod.go.jp/j/press/kisha/2019/02/26a.html

Ministry of Defense, "Areas of U.S. Forces Japan's Facilities, Zones (Exclusive Use Facilities)" ["在日米軍施設 区域(専用施設)面積"], Government of Japan, March 31, 2022a.

Ministry of Defense, *Defense Programs and Budget of Japan (Overview of Budget Request for Reiwa Year 5)* ["我が国の防衛と予算 （令和5年度概算要求の概要)"], Government of Japan, August 2022b. As of October 11, 2022:
https://www.mod.go.jp/j/yosan/yosan_gaiyo/2023/yosan_20220831.pdf

Ministry of Defense, *National Defense Strategy*, Government of Japan, December 16, 2022c. As of January 27, 2023:
https://www.mod.go.jp/j/approach/agenda/guideline/strategy/pdf/strategy_en.pdf

Ministry of Foreign Affairs, "Reference," image, Government of Japan, undated. As of April 19, 2022:
https://www.mofa.go.jp/mofaj/area/usa/hosho/pdfs/gainenzu.pdf

Ministry of Foreign Affairs, "The SACO Final Report," Government of Japan, December 2, 1996. As of March 23, 2022:
https://www.mofa.go.jp/region/n-america/us/security/96saco1.html

Ministry of Foreign Affairs, "Concept Plan," image, Government of Japan, April 28, 2006a. As of April 19, 2022:
https://www.mofa.go.jp/mofaj/kaidan/g_aso/ubl_06/pdfs/2plus2_map_gai.pdf

Ministry of Foreign Affairs, "Deployment of U.S. PAC-3 to Kadena," Government of Japan, July 20, 2006b. As of March 17, 2022:
https://www.mofa.go.jp/announce/announce/2006/7/0720.html

Ministry of Foreign Affairs, "Japan-U.S. Summit Meeting," Government of Japan, February 22, 2013a. As of October 11, 2022:
https://www.mofa.go.jp/region/n-america/us/pmv_1302/130222_01.html

Ministry of Foreign Affairs, *Consolidation Plan for Facilities and Areas in Okinawa*, Government of Japan, April 2013b. As of April 19, 2022:
https://www.mofa.go.jp/mofaj/area/usa/hosho/pdfs/togo_20130405_en.pdf

"Missile Unit Also on Ishigaki, MOD Considering 2 Companies of 120 People" ["石垣にもミサイル部隊　防衛省、2中隊１２０人検討"], *Ryūkyū Shimpō*, May 13, 2015. As of March 2, 2022:
https://ryukyushimpo.jp/news/prentry-242876.html

"Missile Units to Be Deployed on Ishigakijima Island," *Strait Times*, August 3, 2021. As of February 24, 2022:
https://www.straitstimes.com/asia/east-asia/
missile-units-to-be-deployed-on-ishigakijima-island

Mitsuzumi, Shogo, "All Okinawa's Political Fall in Spotlight After Ishigaki Election," *Asahi Shimbun*, February 28, 2022. As of October 11, 2022:
https://www.asahi.com/ajw/articles/14559893

Mitsuzumi, Shogo, and Daizo Teramoto, "Ishigaki Bylaw Revised in Apparent Bid to Block Referendum," *Asahi Shimbun*, June 29, 2021. As of October 11, 2022:
https://www.asahi.com/ajw/articles/14383626

"Miyako GSDF, Government Starting Construction in January, Accelerating Work Toward Deployment" ["宮古陸自、1月着工　政府、配備に向け作業加速"], *Ryūkyū Shimpō*, October 16, 2017. As of March 3, 2022:
https://ryukyushimpo.jp/news/entry-594302.html

"Miyako Residents Request Defense Bureau to Halt Deployment of GSDF Missile Base as Construction Proceeds Without Ground Reinforcements" ["陸自ミサイル基地配備中止を　宮古島住民が防衛局要請　地盤改良せずに建設へ"], *Ryūkyū Shimpō*, August 27, 2019.

MOD—*See* Ministry of Defense.

MOFA—*See* Ministry of Foreign Affairs.

"Naha District Court Dismisses Lawsuit for Referendum about GSDF Deployment to Ishigaki City," trans. by T&CT and Erin Jones, *Ryūkyū Shimpō*, August 27, 2020. As of October 11, 2022:
http://english.ryukyushimpo.jp/2020/09/02/32626/

Narisawa Kaigo, "MOD Exploring Subsidies for the Mageshima Base Plan, Explanation Expected as Early as Next Week" ["馬毛島基地計画で交付金を検討　防衛省、来週にも説明へ"], *Asahi Shimbun*, December 15, 2021. As of March 2, 2022:
https://www.asahi.com/articles/ASPDG6R6KPDGUTIL058.html?

Narisawa Kaigo, "Ground-Based Aegis Replacement Ship, Consideration of Construction Costs in FY24 Budget and Commissioning at End of FY27" ["陸上イージス代替艦、24年度に建造費計上を検討　27年度末就役へ"], *Asahi Shimbun*, September 2, 2022. As of October 11, 2022:
https://www.asahi.com/articles/ASQ9251NJQ80UTIL04H.html

"'Objection' of Nishinoomote City Mayor Fading to Mageshima Base Plan, 'Concerns About Consent or Lack of Consent Fostering Divisions Among Residents'" ["馬毛島基地計画　西之表市長から消えた「不同意」「同意の可否、市民の分断助長する心配がある」"], *Minami Nippon Shimbun*, February 5, 2022. As of October 17, 2022:
https://373news.com/_news/storyid/150987/

Okada Shōhei, "Public Referendum on GSDF Deployment in Ishigaki, Okinawa, Court Does Not Approve Yet Again" ["沖縄・石垣の陸自配備めぐる住民投票　二審も認めず"], *Asahi Shimbun*, March 23, 2021. As of October 12, 2022:
https://www.asahi.com/articles/ASP3R64KLP3RTIPE01M.html

Okinawa Prefecture Planning Department, "Figure II-2-76," in *11th Okinawa Prefectural Residents' Opinion Poll* [第 11回県民意識調査], March 2022. As of April 16, 2023:
https://www.pref.okinawa.jp/site/kikaku/chosei/seido/documents/03-2.pdf

"Okinawa Sues Tokyo in Latest Bid to Stop US Base Relocation," Voice of America, December 25, 2015. As of March 22, 2022:
https://www.voanews.com/a/okinawa-sues-tokyo-in-bid-to-stop-us-base-relocation/3118812.html

"Okinawa: Tokyo to Overrule Referendum on U.S. Base," BBC, February 25, 2019. As of March 16, 2022:
https://www.bbc.com/news/world-asia-47353504

Okumura, Satoshi, "New Training Site for U.S. Military Aircraft Opposed by Local Mayor," *Asahi Shimbun*, October 8, 2020. As of October 12, 2022:
https://www.asahi.com/ajw/articles/13799566

Onaga Takeshi, "The Governor of Okinawa Revoked the Reclamation Approval for the New U.S. Base at Henoko on Oct 13th, 2015," Okinawa Prefectural Government Washington, D.C. Office, October 13, 2015. As of April 4, 2022:
http://dc-office.org/wp-content/uploads/2016/11/The-governor-of-Okinawa-revoked-the-reclamation-approval-for-the-new-U.S.-base-at-Henoko-on-Oct-13th2015.pdf

Ong, Tong, "US Army Opens Patriot Missile Storage Facility in Japan," *Defense Post*, May 26, 2021. As of March 17, 2022:
https://www.thedefensepost.com/2021/05/26/us-patriot-missile-storage-facility-japan/

"Osprey, Provisional Use of Saga Airport Until Henoko Completion" ["オスプレイ、佐賀空港使用 辺野古完成まで暫定"], *Ryūkyū Shimpō*, July 23, 2014. As of March 17, 2022:
https://ryukyushimpo.jp/news/prentry-228940.html

Pajon, Celine, "Understanding the Issue of U.S. Military Bases in Okinawa," Institut Français des Relations Internationals, June 2010. As of March 23, 2022:
https://www.ifri.org/sites/default/files/atoms/files/understanding_the_issue_of_u.s._military_bases_in_okinawa.pdf

Pollack, Andrew, "Okinawans Send Message to Tokyo and U.S. to Cut Bases," *New York Times*, September 9, 1996. As of March 22, 2022:
https://www.nytimes.com/1996/09/09/world/okinawans-send-message-to-tokyo-and-us-to-cut-bases.html

Pollmann, Mina, "Japan Troop Deployment Near Taiwan Clears Major Hurdle," *The Diplomat*, February 25, 2015. As of February 24, 2022:
https://thediplomat.com/2015/02/japan-troop-deployment-near-taiwan-clears-major-hurdle/

"Protest by Opposition Faction of Residents on Miyako to Full Start of Construction of GSDF Garrison" ["陸自駐屯地の本格工事に着手 宮古島市 反対派住民は抗議"], *Ryūkyū Shimpō*, November 20, 2017. As of March 3, 2022:
https://ryukyushimpo.jp/news/entry-616661.html

Rabson, Steve, "Henoko and the U.S. Military: A History of Dependence and Resistance," *Asia-Pacific Journal*, Vol. 10, Iss. 4, No. 2, January 16, 2012. As of April 4, 2022:
https://apjjf.org/2012/10/4/Steve-Rabson/3680/article.html

"Resolution on GSDF Deployment Is 'Tyranny,' Gathering of Residents on Ishigaki Criticize City Assembly" ["陸自配備決議は「横暴」 石垣で集会 市民ら市議会批判"], *Ryūkyū Shimpō*, September 30, 2016. As of March 2, 2022:
https://ryukyushimpo.jp/news/entry-366781.html

Robson, Seth, and Hana Kusumoto, "Possible Deployment of US Reaper Drones Irks Residents of City in Southern Japan," *Stars and Stripes*, February 9, 2022a. As of February 11, 2022:
https://www.stripes.com/theaters/asia_pacific/2022-02-08/mq-9-reaper-hunter-killer-drones-kanoya-air-base-japan-4856311.html

Robson, Seth, and Hana Kusumoto, "Reluctant Mayor OKs U.S. Military Drones in Southern Japan," *Stars and Stripes*, July 13, 2022b. As of October 11, 2022:
https://www.stripes.com/branches/air_force/2022-07-13/reaper-air-force-japan-mayor-6636826.html

"Saga Citizens and JCP Protest Against Promotion of Osprey Deployment to Local Airport," *Japan Press Weekly*, July 5, 2017. As of March 17, 2022:
https://www.japan-press.co.jp/modules/news/index.php?id=10748

"Saga City Disapproves of Use of Saga Airport for Ospreys," *Japan Press Weekly*, August 21, 2014. As of March 17, 2022:
https://www.japan-press.co.jp/modules/news/index.php?id=7476

"Saga Pref. to Accept GSDF's Osprey Deployment," Nippon.com, August 24, 2018. As of March 17, 2022:
https://www.nippon.com/en/news/yjj2018082400707/

"Saga Residents Protest Against Plan to Deploy Ospreys to Local Airport," *Japan Press Weekly*, July 23, 2014. As of March 17, 2022:
https://www.japan-press.co.jp/modules/news/index.php?id=7409

"Saga Residents Want Their Local Airport to Stay Free from Fisheries-Threatening Ospreys," *Japan Press Weekly*, July 27, 2017. As of March 17, 2022:
https://www.japan-press.co.jp/modules/news/index.php?id=10808

Sakaguchi, Seiko, "A Report from Miyako Island: What Is Happening on the Small Islands of Okinawa?" *EcoJesuit*, June 30, 2019. As of February 28, 2022:
https://www.ecojesuit.com/a-report-from-miyako-island-what-is-happening-on-the-small-islands-of-okinawa/

Sato, Daisuke, "U.S. Army Opens Patriot Missile Storage Facility in Japan," *Defence Blog*, May 26, 2021. As of March 17, 2022:
https://defence-blog.com/u-s-army-opens-patriot-missile-storage-facility-in-japan/

Security Consultative Committee, "U.S.-Japan Alliance: Transformation and Realignment for the Future," U.S. Department of State, October 29, 2005. As of April 19, 2022:
https://2001-2009.state.gov/documents/organization/55886.pdf

Security Consultative Committee, "United States-Japan Roadmap for Realignment Implementation," U.S. Department of State, May 1, 2006. As of April 19, 2022:
https://www.mofa.go.jp/region/n-america/us/security/scc/doc0605.html

Security Consultative Committee, "Progress on the Realignment of U.S. Forces in Japan," Ministry of Foreign Affairs, Government of Japan, June 21, 2011. As of October 12, 2022:
https://www.mofa.go.jp/region/n-america/us/security/pdfs/joint1106_02.pdf

Security Consultative Committee, "Joint Statement," Ministry of Foreign Affairs, Government of Japan, April 27, 2012. As of April 19, 2022:
https://www.mofa.go.jp/region/n-america/us/security/scc/pdfs/joint_120427_en.pdf

SSFM International, "Patriot Missile Storage Facility," webpage, undated. As of March 17, 2022:
https://www.ssfm.com/project/patriot-missile-storage-facility/

"Suggesting Approximately 800 SDF Personnel Deployed to Miyako, Meeting Between Vice Defense Minister Satō and Mayor Shimoji" ["宮古島に自衛隊約８００人配備打診 左藤防衛副大臣、下地市長面談"], *Ryūkyū Shimpō*, May 11, 2015. As of March 3, 2022:
https://ryukyushimpo.jp/news/prentry-242804.html

Sumida, Chiyomi, and Matthew Burke, "Okinawa Governor Loses Battle in Base-Relocation War," *Stars and Stripes*, September 16, 2016. As of March 22, 2022:
https://www.stripes.com/news/okinawa-governor-loses-battle-in-base-relocation-war-1.429347

Sumida, Chiyomi, and Megan McCloskey, "U.S. Confirms Patriot Missiles Will Go to Kadena," *Stars and Stripes*, July 16, 2006. As of March 17, 2022:
https://www.stripes.com/news/u-s-confirms-patriot-missiles-will-go-to-kadena-1.51853

Takahashi, Sugio, and Eric Sayers, "America and Japan in a Post-INF World," *War on the Rocks*, March 8, 2019. As of January 27, 2023:
https://warontherocks.com/2019/03/america-and-japan-in-a-post-inf-world/

Takayoshi Igarashi, "Reclamation, Licensing, and the Law: Japan's Courts Take Up the Henoko Base Issue," trans. by Sandi Aritza, *Asia-Pacific Journal*, Vol. 14, Iss. 1, No. 2, January 1, 2016. As of March 23, 2022:
https://apjjf.org/2016/01/2-Igarashi.html

Tamaki Denny, "Message from the Governor," Okinawa Prefectural Government Washington D.C. Office, undated. As of March 10, 2022:
https://dc-office.org/message

Tasevski, Olivia, "Okinawa's Vocal Anti-U.S. Military Base Movement," *The Interpreter*, February 17, 2022. As of March 16, 2022:
https://www.lowyinstitute.org/the-interpreter/okinawa-s-vocal-anti-US-military-base-movement

"'Temporary' Deployment of JSDF Osprey Aircraft to Kisarazu Base Starts," *Japan Press Weekly*, July 11, 2020. As of March 17, 2022:
https://www.japan-press.co.jp/s/news/?id=13054

Tiezzi, Shannon, "Japan to Station Troops on Yonaguni, Near Disputed Islands," *The Diplomat*, April 19, 2014. As of February 28, 2022:
https://thediplomat.com/2014/04/
japan-to-station-troops-on-yonaguni-near-disputed-islands/

Tong, Sheryl Lee Tian, "'Our Land, Our Life': Okinawans Hold Out Against New U.S. Base in Coastal Zone," *Mongabay*, November 25, 2021. As of March 16, 2022:
https://news.mongabay.com/2021/11/
our-land-our-life-okinawans-hold-out-against-new-u-s-base-in-coastal-zone/

"'Toward the Repeal of the Mageshima Base Plan,' Opposing Resident Group of Nishinoomote Submits 24,000 Signatures to the MOD" ["馬毛島基地計画の撤回を」西之表の市民団体が反対署名2万4000筆を防衛省に提出"], Yahoo Japan, February 5, 2022. As of October 14, 2022:
https://news.yahoo.co.jp/articles/793d22c82280a3dc0
bbac4245aa13f053c665c14?fbclid=IwAR3kuKrbYoiIr
a_f_pd3s6DNRFp0IY37kA5gPdpWMgGGe6RlH1N2YTRBPp4

"U.S. Bolsters Missile-Defense Presence in Japan," Military.com, December 26, 2014. As of March 11, 2022:
https://www.military.com/dodbuzz/2014/12/26/
u-s-bolsters-missile-defense-presence-in-japan

U.S. Department of Defense, "Second Missile Defense Radar Deployed to Japan," press release, December 26, 2014.

U.S. Department of State, "Joint Statement of the U.S.-Japan Security Consultative Committee ('2+2')," January 6, 2022.

"U.S. Forcibly Begins X-Radar Construction in Kyoto," *Japan Press Weekly*, May 28, 2014. As of March 11, 2022:
https://www.japan-press.co.jp/modules/news/index.php?id=7238

U.S. Government Accountability Office, *Marine Corps Asia Pacific Realignment: DOD Should Resolve Capability Deficiencies and Infrastructure Risks and Revise Cost Estimates*, GAO-17-415, April 2017.

U.S. Mission Japan, "Joint Statement of the Security Consultative Committee (2+2)," January 11, 2023.

"U.S. Spy Drones Likely to Be Deployed to Western Japan Air Base," *Japan News*, January 27, 2022. As of March 10, 2022:
https://the-japan-news.com/news/article/0008218922

"Vice Defense Minister Requests Miyako Survey of GSDF Deployment" ["防衛副大臣、陸自配備で宮古島調査を要請"], *Ryūkyū Shimpō*, June 13, 2014. As of March 2, 2022:
https://ryukyushimpo.jp/news/prentry-226911.html

Vowell, J. B., and Kevin Joyce, "The U.S. Army Can Be the Joint Force's Contact Layer in the Pacific," *Defense One*, January 9, 2023. As of January 27, 2023:
https://www.defenseone.com/ideas/2023/01/
army-can-be-contact-layer-western-pacific/381631/

Yamaguchi, Mari, "Tokyo Sues Okinawa in U.S. Base Relocation Dispute," *Air Force Times*, November 17, 2015a. As of March 22, 2022:
https://www.airforcetimes.com/news/your-military/2015/11/17/
tokyo-sues-okinawa-in-u-s-base-relocation-dispute/

Yamaguchi, Mari, "Okinawa Officials Sue to Stop Move of Marine Corps Air Station Futenma," *Defense News*, December 25, 2015b. As of March 22, 2022:
https://www.defensenews.com/news/your-navy/2015/12/25/
okinawa-officials-sue-to-stop-move-of-marine-corps-air-station-futenma/

Yamaguchi, Mari, "Tens of Thousands Rally for Removal of Marine Base on Okinawa," *Marine Corps Times*, August 12, 2018. As of March 10, 2022:
https://www.marinecorpstimes.com/news/your-marine-corps/2018/08/12/
tens-of-thousands-rally-for-removal-of-marine-base-on-okinawa/

Yamaguchi, Mari, "Okinawa Governor Renews Demand to Stop Marine Corps' Futenma Base Relocation Plan," *Marine Corps Times*, December 26, 2019. As of March 10, 2022:
https://www.marinecorpstimes.com/news/your-marine-corps/2019/12/27/
okinawa-governor-renews-demand-to-stop-marine-corps-futenma-base-relocation-plan/

Yamaguchi, Mari, "Japan Confirms It's Scrapping U.S. Missile Defense System," *Defense News*, June 25, 2020. As of April 4, 2022:
https://www.defensenews.com/land/2020/06/25/
japan-confirms-its-scrapping-us-missile-defense-system/

Yeo, Mike, "Japan Suspends Aegis Ashore Deployment, Pointing to Cost and Technical Issues," *Defense News*, June 15, 2020. As of April 4, 2020:
https://www.defensenews.com/global/asia-pacific/2020/06/15/japan-suspends-aegis-ashore-deployment-pointing-to-cost-and-technical-issues/

Yun-hyung Gil, "Japanese Community with THAAD Radar Glumly Says 'It's OK,'" *Hankyoreh*, July 18, 2016. As of March 15, 2022:
https://english.hani.co.kr/arti/english_edition/e_international/752843.html